CINCINNATI REDS® Scrapbook

BY BOB RATHGEBER

JCP
CORP. OF VIRGINIA

Library of Congress Catalog Number 81-80979

ISBN 0-938694-05-7

Copyright 1982 by JCP Corp. of Virginia. All rights reserved. No part of this book may be reproduced in any form without written permission from the publisher. Direct inquiries to:

JCP Corp. of Virginia
P.O. Box 814
Virginia Beach, Virginia
23451

Book and dustjacket design by W. Bradley Miller

Other titles from JCP Corp. of Virginia and its associated firm, Jordan & Company, Publishers, Inc.:

The Baltimore Colts: A Pictorial History

The Washington Redskins: A Pictorial History

The Cincinnati Reds: A Pictorial History of Professional Baseball's Oldest Team

The Los Angeles Dodgers: The First Twenty Years

The Pittsburgh Pirates: A Century Old Baseball Tradition

The Winning Tradition: A Pictorial History of Carolina Basketball

The Pittsburgh Steelers: A Pictorial History

He Ain't No Bum By O. A. "Bum" Phillips and Ray Buck

The Trojan Heritage: A Pictorial History of USC Football

The New England Patriots: A Pictorial History

The Philadelphia Phillies: A Pictorial History

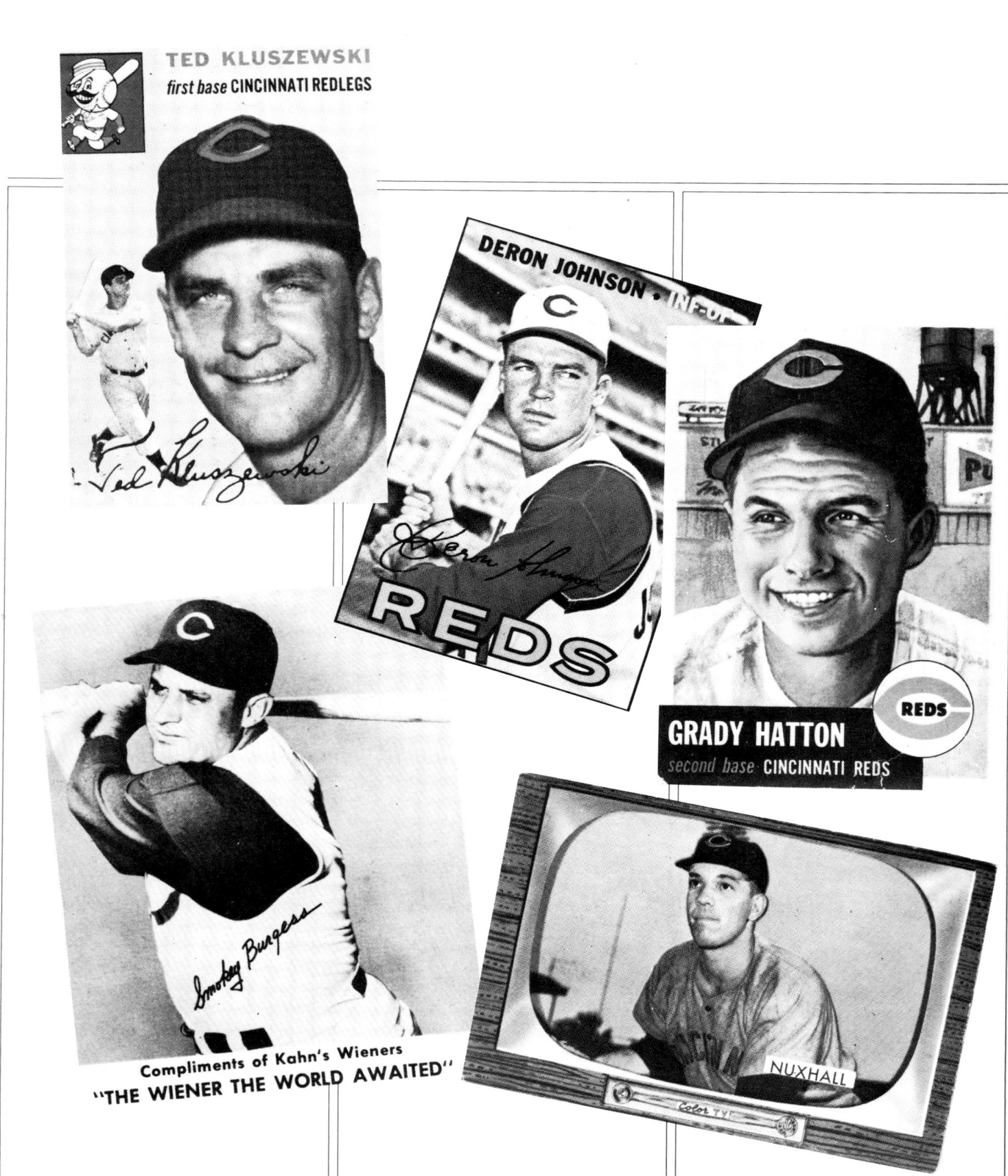

FROM THE AUTHOR

This book was on the drawing board for a long time. I first started thinking about such a volume in 1974...

[text partially obscured by overlapping red card]

...edited the copy, making English out of a few Chinese sentences, and was there when I needed a boost during a couple of those dreary, cold February days when it looked like baseball season would never come again.

...thanks goes to several ...he Cincinnati Reds who ...along on this project — ...irector Jim Ferguson and ...Dorcas Patten, and ...the club's vice president...rketing.

...rouble ever again walking into the library of *The Cincinnati Enquirer* if I didn't thank Fred Morganer and his staff for their help. They pulled many pounds of newspaper clippings from the files for my research.

I could not have written this book nearly as easily, either, had it not been for Lee Allen's book, *The Cincinnati Reds*. It was published in 1948 and it helped to provide me with a tremendous amount of background information that was used. And without the *Baseball Encyclopedia*, the chore would have been mammoth.

There are thousands of stories that could be told in a Cincinnati Reds Scrapbook. I believe the 64 which follow are an excellent representation of more than 100 years of Cincinnati Reds baseball history.

Bob Rathgeber

Bob Rathgeber and his family moved to Florida when he was a high school senior. He graduated from Palmetto High in Palmetto, Florida. He attended Manatee Junior College in Bradenton, Florida, and, at the same time, began a journalism career with *The Bradenton (Fla.) Herald*. He moved to Lakeland, Florida, in 1967 and the following year he was named sports editor of *The Lakeland Ledger*. At age 21, he was the youngest sports editor of a daily paper in the state. In 1970 he moved to Cincinnati and became the assistant publicity director of the Cincinnati Reds. In 1975 he was named director of publications.

He joined *The Enquirer* in March 1979 as a sports copy editor.

He and his wife Karon have two sons, Bo, 12, and Mike, 10, and a dog named Ralph. They reside in the Cincinnati suburb of White Oak.

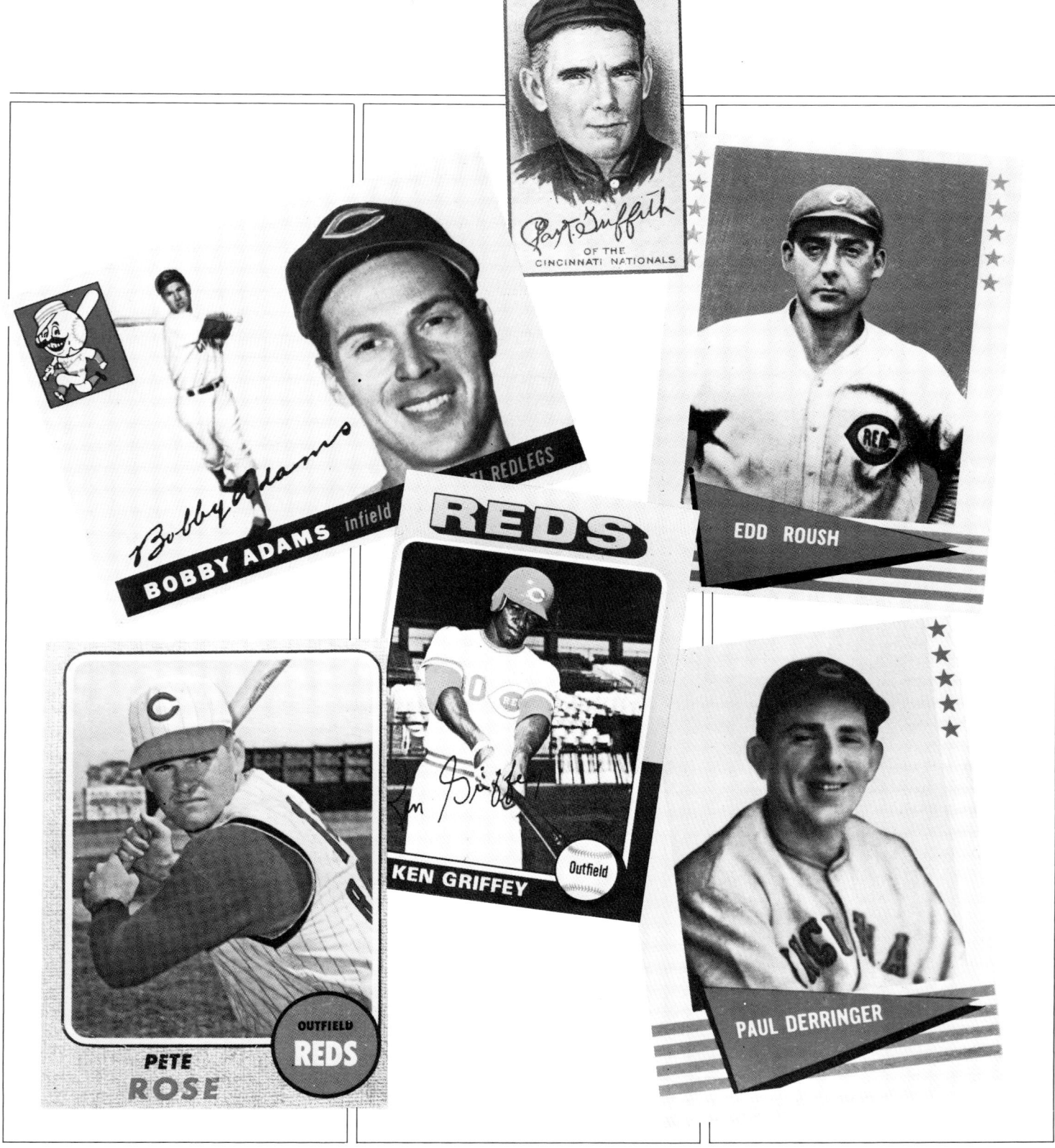

FOREWORD

Since 1974 I've been broadcasting Cincinnati Reds baseball. It has been a very pleasurable experience for the most part, because these past nine years, for a team so rich in history and tradition, have been the club's most successful. Division titles, pennants, back-to-back world championships. They're all team accomplishments and all very exciting. The individuals who have been a part of these great Reds teams also have been exciting. Individuals like Pete Rose, Joe Morgan, Johnny Bench, Dave Concepcion, Tony Perez, Sparky Anderson, John McNamara, Tom Seaver, George Foster, Clay Carroll, Ken Griffey, Dave Collins. The list could go on and on and on.

For the same nine years I've hosted a program entitled "The Cincinnati Reds Radio Scrapbook" which recounts interesting events and tells of individuals who have been a part of the great history of this team dating back to its beginning in 1869 as the first of all professional baseball teams. This book is an extension, imprinted words and pictures, of those radio programs.

When I was asked to write this foreword for the *Cincinnati Reds Scrapbook,* I decided to do so for several reasons.

One reason is the book's author, Bob Rathgeber. For a number of years, Bob researched and wrote "The Reds Radio Scrapbook" that I

voiced on the air. He's a walking encyclopedia of the history of Reds baseball. He's also an accomplished writer. Most important of all, he's a good friend.

Secondly, my opportunity to learn, through The Reds Radio Scrapbook, about the history of the Reds and its great players has been entertaining and helpful. I've found that Reds fans are unique— they not only are interested in Reds teams of today, but they also are proud of the teams of the past. The good times and the bad —enjoy remembering them, if you will. For that reason, this book is necessary.

As you turn the pages, you'll find it's all here. The 1869 Red Stockings, led by Harry and George Wright, who won 130 consecutive games. The 1919 team that brought Cincinnati its first world championship, a team that featured players like Edd Roush and Hiney Grove. Back-to-back pennants in 1939 and 1940 and a world championship victory over Detroit in 1940. Those teams were blessed with the likes of Paul Derringer and Bucky Walters. There were Johnny Vander Meer's back-to-back no-hit games, and Ernie Lombardi and Frank McCormick. The powerful 1956 team that tied a National League record by hitting 221 home runs. The 1961 ragamuffin team, managed by the fiery Fred Hutchinson, that came out of nowhere and captured the NL pennant. Frank Robinson, Joe Nuxhall, Crosley Field to Riverfront Stadium. Bob Howsam, Dick Wagner. The team of the 70s. You'll find the big games and the not-so-big ones, all playing a most definite part in the history of the Cincinnati Reds.

And I'm sure that no matter how knowledgeable you may be about the Reds, you'll find, on reading this book, that there are many things that you didn't know. That's what makes it so truly interesting.

The *Cincinnati Reds Scrapbook.* Enjoy.

Marty Brennaman

CONTENTS

THE STADIUMS 12

The English
Founder Of The Pros
HARRY WRIGHT 20

The First
Big Hitter In The Game
GEORGE WRIGHT 22

The First Pitch
That Curved
CANDY CUMMINGS 24

The Early King
Of Second Basemen
BID McPHEE 26

From A No-Hitter
To Nowhere
BUMPUS JONES 28

A Strong Arm,
A Perfect Player
BUCK EWING 30

The Birth
Of Umpires' Signals
WILLIAM "DUMMY" HOY 32

The Pitch
That Killed A Career
FRANK "NOODLES" HAHN ... 34

When Hitting
Became A Science
CY SEYMOUR 36

A Pitching
Trade That Backfired
CHRISTY MATHEWSON 38

The High Price
Of A League War
SAM CRAWFORD 40

A Stolen Base
That Was Found
BOB BESCHER 42

The Father
Of The World Series
GARRY HERRMANN 44

From A Flooded
Field To The Flag
PAT MORAN 46

A Mean Bat
And A Mean Negotiator
EDD ROUSH 48

The Pitching
"Virginia Gentleman"
EPPA RIXEY 52

A Latin Temper
On The Mound
ADOLFO LUQUE 54

Lights Out
For The Shine Ball
HOD ELLER 56

Quick Hands
And Temper At Third
BABE PINELLI 58

From College
To Pros And Back
ETHAN ALLEN 60

The Long Wait
Behind The Plate
BUBBLES HARGRAVE 62

The Two Who
Shared Left Field
BRESSLER/CHRISTENSEN 64

The Great
Pinch-Hitting Pitcher
RED LUCAS 66

Who Turned On
The Lights?
LARRY MACPHAIL 68

When Babe Was Almost A Player
HARRY STEVENS 70

When Babe
Was Almost A Manager
LARRY MACPHAIL 72

When The Reds
Ink Turned Black
POWEL CROSLEY 74

The Night
The Lights Came On
MAY 24, 1935, GAME 76

A First-Base
Prize That Got Away
JOHNNY MIZE 78

The Builder
Of The "Roughhouse"
CHARLES DRESSEN 80

How A Commissioner
Was Picked
WARREN GILES 82

The Manager
Who Read The Book
DEACON BILL
  McKECHNIE 84

A No-Hitter
Follows A No-Hitter
JOHNNY VANDER MEER 88

To The Mound By Way Of Third BUCKY WALTERS 90	The Strongest Man In Baseball TED KLUSZEWSKI 114	When Hustle Won An All-Star Game PETE ROSE 134
The Kickin' That Overcame Lickin' PAUL DERRINGER 92	How A Home-Run Order Was Filled SMOKY BURGESS 116	"Some Kind Of Man" And Manager SPARKY ANDERSON 136
A First-Class Player On Third BILL WERBER 94	Center Field, Center Of Attention GUS BELL 118	Five Gold Gloves At Short DAVE CONCEPCION 138
The Backstop Who's Overlooked ERNIE LOMBARDI 96	A Swing Hitched To Stardom FRANK ROBINSON 120	The Occasional Home-Run Hitter HAL KING 140
A Catcher's Call And Tragedy WILLARD HERSHBERGER 98	The Man Who Managed To The End FRED HUTCHINSON 122	The Slugging Second Sackers KAMPOURIS/MORGAN 142
The Coach Who Caught The Series JIMMIE WILSON 100	Little League To Major League JOEY JAY 124	A Catcher's Hit That Wasn't Caught JOHNNY BENCH 144
Lucky No. 7, The Fantastic Game 1940 WORLD SERIES 102	The Era Of The Dancing Knuckler BOB PURKEY 126	The Best World Series Ever Played GAME NO. 7 — 1975 146
A Javelin That Was Thrown Away JOE BEGGS 104	A Pen As Mighty As A Bat JIM BROSNAN 128	The Man Is Terrific TOM SEAVER 148
The Star Who Lost To Gary Cooper WAITE HOYT 106	A Brief Stop At Second In '61 JIM BAUMER 130	INDEX 150
The Youngest Pitcher Of Them All JOE NUXHALL 108	Man's Best Friend TONY PEREZ 132	
The Whip That Cracked For A Season EWELL BLACKWELL 110		
The Man Who Broke A Barrier CHUCK HARMON 112		

Riverfront Stadium, the newest and by far the largest ballpark ever built in Cincinnati, opened for baseball in June 1970.

The history of baseball in Cincinnati dates back to the 1850s when a young man from the Mt. Auburn area of Cincinnati named William Howard Taft had aspirations of becoming a baseball player. Games in those days were played in open fields and on cricket grounds. One of the first recorded official playing-sites in Cincinnati was on the city's west side. Games were played in the area where Union Terminal, an old railroad station turned into a shopping center, now stands. Later professional games were played on the city's north side near Spring Grove Cemetery.

In 1884 a ballpark finally was constructed at the corner of Findlay and Western avenues in the west end, and it became a home for the Cincinnati Reds for more than 85 years.

It wasn't Crosley Field then, or even Redland Field. All that was there was a ramshackle wooden grandstand, and the batters even batted into the sun, which made hitting quite difficult in the late afternoon.

The Palace
of the Fans
1902

This artist's drawing of Redland Field appeared in the dedication program in May of 1912.

Ten years later the field was changed. A new grandstand was erected and batters no longer had to look into the sun when facing the pitcher. Right field instead became the trouble spot with ole' sol.

In 1900 fire destroyed the grandstand which necessitated the return of home plate to the right field area. It was a temporary move, however, as a new, elegant stand was built shortly thereafter.

This new ballpark was called the "Palace of the Fans," and in its day it was majestic. In 1912, after further additions, the field was renamed Redland Field.

From 1912 until the late 1930s, when the Reds won the National League pennant, the ballpark remained virtually the same. Indeed, the name changed to Crosley Field when Powel Crosley Jr. purchased the team in the early 1930s, but there were no physical changes in the structure until the grandstand was double-decked down both foul lines in 1939. This was completed in time to accommodate the big crowds attending the World Series.

Crosley Field holds many memories for baseball fans in Cincinnati: the flood in 1937 when pitchers Lee Grissom and Gene Schott rowed a boat over the center-field fence; baseball's first night game, in 1935, when President Franklin D. Roosevelt threw a switch in the White House to turn on the lights; the goat run in right field and the moon deck and the

Crosley Field was almost completely submerged when flood waters from the Mill Creek spread throughout the Mill Creek Valley in January of 1937.

CINCINNATI REDS Scrapbook

The English Founder Of The Pros
HARRY WRIGHT

Harry Wright was to baseball what George Washington was to the United States. Wright was "first in baseball" as the founder of professional play. He put together the first all-pro team in Cincinnati in 1869.

Wright was a native of Sheffield, England. He emigrated to America as a youngster, coming with his father who was a highly regarded cricket player.

Harry spent his youth in the New York City area and, like his father, became a professional cricket player. He first saw baseball played in 1857 in Hoboken, New Jersey, and the game immediately fascinated him.

The next year Wright joined the New York Knickerbockers, an amateur baseball team, and he played in the East until 1865 when he moved to Cincinnati to set up a cricket club.

Baseball had caught on in Cincinnati during the early 1860s. Among those who played daily as a teen-ager was a boy named William Howard Taft. The name should be familiar. He would later become President of the United States and Chief Justice of the U.S. Supreme Court.

When Wright arrived in Cincinnati, he found a number of thriving baseball clubs. The two best teams were the Buckeyes and the Red Stockings. In 1868 Wright was offered the managership of the Red Stockings. He brought in four paid players from the East and the following year he established the first all-professional baseball team.

The highest paid of the 10 team members was Wright's younger brother George who gave up a career as an engraver to earn $1,400 a year as a baseball player.

Harry Wright's first team was literally unbeatable, but it did tie once in that season for a 65-0-1 record. The team played from coast to coast. Printed statistics of that era show the Red Stockings traveled 12,000 miles by rail and boat. More than 200,000 fans watched the 66 games. The Red Stockings outscored their opponents by a whopping 2,395 to 575. George Wright batted .518 and hit 59 home runs in the 52 games he played.

Everybody appeared to be excited about the new professional team except the hometown newspaper, *The Cincinnati Enquirer*. After a game on April 17, which opened the home season, *The Enquirer* opined:

"The baseball season for 1869 opened yesterday by a game between the first nine of the Cincinnati Club and the field. The playing on both sides was very poor. There was quite a large number of spectators present, but the enthusiasm of last summer was lacking."

The story didn't bother to mention a score of the game.

As the season progressed, the Red Stockings scheduled an important game in New York against the Mutuals, the best club in the East. The Reds won the game, 4-2, a remarkable score since most teams of that era reached double figures.

Cincinnati baseball fans were excited and anxiously awaited the outcome of this game. It was reported that about 2,000 fans milled around the old Gibson Hotel in downtown Cincinnati, awaiting the result. When the Western Union office reported the winning score, the crowd reaction is said to have sounded like the Fourth of July.

At a banquet when the club returned, Aaron Champion, the president of the Red Stockings, was obviously ecstatic.

"Someone asked me today who I would rather be — President Ulysses S. Grant or President Champion of the Cincinnati Baseball Club. I immediately answered him that I would by far rather be the president of the baseball club," Champion said.

Other teams began employing professional players and soon the original Red Stockings broke up. Even Harry Wright left Cincinnati, taking over a team in Boston after the 1870 season. He later moved to Providence and then to Philadelphia.

Wright compiled a lifetime winning percentage of .610 and retired after the 1893 season. Two years later the man who brought professional baseball to Cincinnati and brought fame to the Cincinnati Red Stockings died at the age of 60.

Harry Wright was the founding father of the Cincinnati Red Stockings, baseball's first all-professional team, in 1869.

The First Big Hitter In The Game
GEORGE WRIGHT

In professional baseball's infancy, probably the best player in the game was George Wright, a 5-foot-9-inch, 150-pound infielder. All accounts produce the profile of a player far ahead of his time, a player with skills considerably more advanced than his contemporaries.

He was a natural to come to Cincinnati to be the shortstop on the 1869 Cincinnati Red Stockings, baseball's first all-professional team. The manager was George's brother, Harry Wright.

George Wright had gained quite a reputation in the East as a young cricket player, proclaimed as one of the best in the world at the age of 16 in 1863. Three years later he was recognized as one of the best baseball players. He began a career with the Olympics in New York and his reputation spread far and wide.

When older brother Harry founded the Red Stockings, one of the first players contacted was George Wright. He moved to Cincinnati from Morrissiana, New York, and became the top-paid professional player — earning a first-year salary of $1,400.

George Wright was an incredible hitter. When the Red Stockings played from coast to coast in 1869, traveling more than 12,000 miles, Wright was the team's primary gate attraction and the game's first great hitter. In 52 games, George Wright batted .518, scored 339 runs and hit 59 home runs. Granted, the game wasn't played as it is today, but the team as a whole produced only 169 home runs and Wright hit 59 of them.

George Wright stayed in Cincinnati through 1870 and moved on to Boston in 1871 when the National Association of Professional Baseball Clubs was formed. That association was the forerunner of the National League, founded five years later.

George Wright eventually played seven seasons in the National League with Boston and Providence, Rhode Island. His last year was 1882. Then he embarked on another career that made him almost as famous as did his baseball playing.

George Wright opened a sporting goods store with a partner, founding the Wright and Ditson Sporting Goods Company.

Soon after opening his store, Wright placed an order for some cricket bats through a firm in Scotland. While leafing through the Scottish catalogue, an advertisement for golf clubs caught his eye.

Golf was still unknown to American sport and it intrigued Wright. Eventually, he was sent a rule book. Soon after that, Wright and a group of his sporting friends laid out a nine-hole golf course near Boston.

The following year the prestigious Brookline Country Club began promoting the new game and the sport officially was introduced to America's sportsdom.

Wright lived to see baseball and golf change dramatically. He was still around in 1936 when the Baseball Hall of Fame was founded. The following year, at the age of 90, Wright died, but not before being recognized by the Hall of Fame as one of the game's greats. He was one of the first members inducted into this exclusive Valhalla of baseball's heroes.

Standing: Hurley, Sub.; G. Wright, S.S.; Allison, C.; McVey, R.F.; Leonard, L.F. Sitting: Sweasy, 2nd Base; Waterman, 3rd Base; H. Wright, C.F.; Brainard, P.; Gould, 1st Base.

George Wright was baseball's first star. A big hitter and a top gate-attraction, Wright later helped launch another game new to America — golf.

The First Pitch That Curved
CANDY CUMMINGS

If this pitcher could have patented his invention, he would have become a millionaire. Instead, the one-time Cincinnati Reds hurler is lost in time and only the most studious baseball historians are familiar with Arthur "Candy" Cummings.

Cummings' invention was the curve ball. For four seasons, 1872-1875, when he pitched for the New York Mutuals, Baltimore, Philadelphia, and Hartford, he was the best pitcher in the United States.

Candy Cummings made his discovery while throwing clam shells as a youngster in Ware, Massachusetts.

"It was in the '60s that I discovered the curve ball, and strange to say, it was the idle throwing of half a clam shell that gave birth to such an idea," Cummings told a Massachusetts newspaper reporter just before the turn of the century.

When Cummings threw the clam shells, he became fascinated by their snakelike course through the air. He theorized that a baseball could be made to perform in the same fashion when it was thrown with the proper spin.

The idea of a curving baseball at first seemed far-fetched to a lot of people, but Cummings wasn't dismayed.

"I was laughed at by scientific men and baseball experts," Cummings said in his interview.

"But I finally proved to them that the stunt could be done, and for a long time I was known as the boy wonder."

In 1867, two years before the Cincinnati Red Stockings fielded the first all-professional baseball team, Cummings unveiled his curve ball in a game that he pitched for Harvard College.

"At this time with secret practice, I found that I had perfect control of either the drop or rise, which came to me before the out- or in-shoot, because the pitching was done with a perpendicular swing.

"In the Harvard game Archie Bush, whom I feared for his powerful batting, was at bat. Bush swung at the first curve ball pitched, but only came within a foot of connecting. I tried it again and found that he was really at my mercy and I knew that I had succeeded."

Cummings' pitching delivery would look rather awkward and confusing on today's baseball field. Baseball rules in the late 1860s required a pitcher to keep both feet on the ground until the ball had left the hand. The pitching arm had to be kept near the side and the delivery was made with a perpendicular swing. In other words, the pitch was thrown underhanded.

The throwing of the curve ball took its toll on Cummings. He developed baseball's first arm problem.

Cummings reported, "... it was a hard strain as the wrist and second finger had to do all the work. I snapped the ball away from me like a whip and this caused my wrist bone to get out of place quite often. I was compelled to wear a supporter on my wrist all one season on account of this strain."

Cummings began his professional career in 1872 with the New York Mutuals. He won 31 games his first season. He followed up the next year at Baltimore with 27 wins, 30 wins in 1874 at Philadelphia and 35 wins in 1875 at Hartford. By 1876 Cummings had lost his effectiveness with the curve ball — because of the aching arm. He won only 15 games for Hartford that year and moved to Cincinnati the following season. He won only six games against 14 losses that season and that finished off his major league career at the age of 29.

Although Cummings played only six seasons in the major leagues, he has a spot in Cooperstown alongside Ruth and Gehrig and DiMaggio and Williams. His Hall of Fame plaque reads, "Pitched first curve ball in baseball history."

Candy Cummings invented the curve ball and gained a spot in baseball's Hall of Fame.

The Early King Of Second Basemen BID McPHEE

Most Cincinnati Reds fans will assert that Joe Morgan was the best second baseman in the team's long history. Johnny Temple was good, too, but he wasn't in Morgan's class. There were others like Alex Kampouris and Tommy Helms and Hughie Critz — talented, but not sensational.

Before the turn of the century, in an era when baseball was a different game from what it is today, there was a second baseman with the Cincinnati Reds who was in a class by himself among professional baseball players. His name was John Alexander McPhee, affectionately known as Bid McPhee.

McPhee was lauded in his day as the "king bee of second basemen" by Cincinnati fans and by a majority of others scattered around the country.

He had all the skills needed to be a standout, and the Reds were once offered the sensational sum of $10,000 by Cap Anson for McPhee's contract. He held the Cincinnati career record for most hits until a fellow named Pete Rose broke it some 70 years later. He once stole 96 bases in one season and had more than 700 in his career. He set a fielding mark that stood for 29 years.

And he did that without wearing a glove in the field.

Bid McPhee was one of the last major league infielders to begin using a leather fielding aid, and he did it only in the final three years of his career — after setting a one-season fielding mark of .982.

McPhee, in an interview in *The Cincinnati Enquirer* on April 12, 1890, said, "No, I never use a glove on either hand in a game. I have never seen the necessity of wearing one; and besides, I cannot hold a thrown ball if there is anything on my hands. This glove business has gone a little too far. It is all wrong to suppose that your hands will get battered out of shape if you don't use them (gloves). True, hot-hit balls do sting a little at the opening of the season, but after you get used to it, there is no trouble on that score."

Born in New York, McPhee was raised in a small Illinois town, played three seasons of minor league baseball in Davenport, Iowa, and Toledo, Ohio, before joining the Reds in 1892. It took a great deal of convincing by the Cincinnati management to persuade McPhee to play baseball. He was an accountant in the off-season and made more money keeping books than the Reds were willing to pay for playing baseball. But Cincinnati upped its ante and McPhee gave up his accounting career.

Bid McPhee spent all 18 of his major league seasons with the Reds. For two years, 1901 and 1902, he was the team's manager. Later, he scouted for Cincinnati. He broke all ties with baseball after the 1909 campaign.

In 1932 an article in *The Sporting News* proclaimed that McPhee had passed to "that great infield in the sky," but all the time he was living in obscurity in Ocean Beach, California, a community near San Diego. "It is not often a man has the pleasure of reading his own obituary," McPhee wrote to *The Sporting News,* telling one and all that he was very much alive.

McPhee lived another 11 years in retirement away from the game he played so well, dying at the age of 83 in 1943.

One can only wonder what he would think today of the huge gloves that adorn the hands of baseball's infielders.

Bid McPhee was the all-time Cincinnati Reds hit leader (2,249) before Pete Rose. And in 1887 he stole 96 bases.

From A No-Hitter To Nowhere
BUMPUS JONES

The 1892 season for the Cincinnati Reds is one of the most interesting in the club's pages of history, especially when Bumpus Jones pitched a no-hitter on the final day of the season.

Charles Comiskey, who later would found the American League and own the Chicago White Sox franchise, was the Cincinnati manager. He had the club playing well in the early season. The Reds had a 44-31 record and were in fourth place in the 12-team National League.

Among the games in the first half of the season was one on June 20 between the Reds and the Chicago Cubs. Pitchers Tony Mullane of the Reds and Addision Gumbert of the Cubs were on the mound. Each pitched all 20 innings of the game, called at 7-7, when the Cubs had to catch a train. When the two clubs started play in the 19th inning, the game became the longest marathon in baseball history, exceeding an 18-inning game between Providence and Detroit.

During the second half of the season the Reds began to struggle. One afternoon in Cincinnati the home club was beaten, 26-6, by Philadelphia. It was such a pitiful game that the Reds played before mostly empty stands the remainder of the season.

Few fans were on hand when the Reds and Pittsburgh's team were set to end the season on October 15. The game was meaningless to the standings. It was one of those "let's get the game over with and get out of here" kind of days that arrive when two teams are wallowing around in the standings during the final stage of the season.

Before the game, a country boy from Xenia, a town in central Ohio, swaggered into the Cincinnati clubhouse and told the Reds that he was a pitcher.

The rules were loose 90 years ago, so Comiskey told this 22-year-old right-hander named Jones to prove it. Comiskey told the youngster that he would be the starting pitcher against Pittsburgh in order to prove his statement. Jones didn't even sign a contract. He was given a uniform, warmed up and took the mound against the Pirates.

Inning after inning Jones amazed the few onlookers. Ending the seventh inning, he hadn't allowed a hit. In the eighth, the Pirates again went hitless. Then came the ninth. Jones again held the Pirates without a base hit, completing one of the most unbelievable no-hit games in baseball history.

After that performance, the Reds immediately gave him a contract and there were great expectations for the next season. But the expectations weren't answered by performance.

Bumpus Jones was a flash in the pan. He pitched only four games for Cincinnati in 1893. He won one and was driven hard from the mound in the others. The Reds released him and the New York club picked him up. He pitched one game, lost it, and never again was heard from in major league baseball history.

Bumpus Jones' baseball career ended just as quickly as it began. But the sound was different: it ended with a whimper, not a boast.

Bumpus Jones pitched a no-hitter in his first start with the Reds and then won only one more game in a short career.

A Strong Arm, A Perfect Player
BUCK EWING

"The death of Buck Ewing removes from the scene of earthly activity the only *absolutely perfect* ball player the writer has ever seen in action in a period of thirty years. He was, in his prime, in all respects, the greatest ball player that ever wore a spiked shoe. He was perfect in all departments and had not a weakness."

Those words were written on October 27, 1906, by an unnamed editor of *Sporting Life*, a sports-oriented weekly newspaper that circulated throughout the East and Midwest in the early 1900s.

Buck Ewing, whom the writer was describing, was a former Cincinnati Reds player and manager. He was such an outstanding player that he was elected to the Hall of Fame in 1939.

Ewing was born near Cincinnati in 1859 and his family moved to the city when he was two years old. He grew up on the city's East Side and played baseball as a youngster when the Cincinnati Red Stockings were being founded as the first all-professional team in the late 1860s. He signed his first professional contract for $85 in 1880.

Although Ewing's best days were with the New York Giants from 1883 to 1890, he continued to be an outstanding player when he was signed by Cincinnati as a player-manager in 1895. He batted .318 as the team's first baseman-manager and for years he had the Reds near the top of the National League standings as their manager.

He was best known as a catcher.

"As a catcher," the *Sporting Life* editor wrote, "he outclassed all we have ever seen. He was a sure catcher, quick on his feet, alert in mind, a splendid coach for a pitcher, a keen reader of batsmen and his swift, accurate throwing was simply perfect.

"In addition, he was a grand batsman, always ranking with the leaders; and as a base runner he ranked always with the best. The player of this generation nearest in calibre to Buck Ewing is Hans Wagner as a batter and base runner and John Kling as a catcher."

Wagner, the Pittsburgh Pirates shortstop, is acknowledged as one of baseball's all-time great hitters while Kling is regarded as one of the best receivers.

Ewing's powerful right arm is said to have been one of the strongest in all of baseball. When he played, his arm was in a class by itself. Frequently, it has been written, he took no step when throwing and never threw from over his shoulder or head, but snapped the ball with a sidearmed swing that made the balls he threw "strike a baseman's hand like a lump of lead."

He had a special play and used it often, hoping to get opposing base runners to challenge his arm. He intentionally would let the pitched ball bounce away from him at the plate, hoping that the runner would try to advance. If the runner did try, most often he easily would be thrown out at second base, a victim of Ewing's sucker tactics and strong arm.

For one season during his playing career, Ewing bolted from the National League and joined the New York team in the Players League, a baseball circuit founded by prominent players in protest over low pay and other shortcomings in the established majors.

While he was with the New York team in the Players League, Ewing displayed some engineering expertise. Ewing was asked to lay out a baseball diamond on an open field that had been located. He did just that. The place later became known as the Polo Grounds. When the New York Mets played there in the early 1960s, the place remained just as Ewing had constructed it, except for modernization along the way.

Buck Ewing, one of baseball's greats, never lived to see his game of baseball progress a lot. Suffering from diabetes and a liver ailment, he died in Cincinnati in 1906 at the age of 47.

Buck Ewing was regarded as one of baseball's all-time finest catchers.

The Pitch That Killed A Career
FRANK "NOODLES" HAHN

He was the Sandy Koufax of his day. He was sensational on the mound, dominating the opposition in nearly every outing. His fastball was the best. He was the strikeout king.

Also like Koufax — the great Dodger pitcher who had no peers when he dominated baseball in the 1960s — this pitcher's career was cut short because of a sore arm.

Newspaper articles referred to this Cincinnati Reds pitcher at the turn of the century as "The Great Hahn." His name was Frank G. Hahn, but to baseball fans 80 years ago he was simply "Noodles."

For six years, 1899-1904, Hahn was as good as, if not better than, many of the pitchers who would go on to gain Hall of Fame status — Jack Chesbro, Cy Young, Rube Waddell and Christy Mathewson.

When he was a 20-year-old rookie in 1899, Hahn won 23 games.

In 1900 at age 21, he pitched a no-hitter against Philadelphia.

In 1901 the Reds finished in last place, but Hahn, 22, won 22 games. He had 233 strikeouts, the most in the National League, and he completed 41 of the 42 games he started.

In one 14-inning game that season, he struck out 16 batters, a Reds record that stood until Jim Maloney tied it in 1963 and then broke it a year later. It was also a league mark that stood until Dizzy Dean struck out 17 hitters in 1933.

Hahn won 22 games in each of the next two years, 1902 and 1903.

In 1904 Hahn's victory total dropped to 16 and he began playing around with a new pitch. The experiment was disastrous. His first choice in 1905 was a spitball. When it was legal, the pitch was an effective weapon for many pitchers. When thrown correctly, the ball would drop suddenly when it reached the plate.

For Hahn, that pitch was the wrong choice. The first time he threw the pitch, he felt something snap in his strong left arm. The once lively left arm went limp and it began aching almost immediately.

He tried to pitch, but the pain was almost unbearable. He worked in only 13 games and pitched just 77 innings. The golden arm was dead. At the "ripe old" age of 26, the Reds released their one-time sure-fire winner.

Hahn tried to come back the following year, signing with the New York American League club, but after six games he called it quits and returned to Cincinnati where be became a government meat inspector.

Even though his playing days were finished, Hahn was a fixture at the Cincinnati ballpark. He pitched batting practice and enjoyed suiting up. He was still doing this at age 61 in 1940.

Noodles Hahn will never make the Hall of Fame, but for six years, when he won 121 games, major league baseball had a Hall-of-Famer.

34

Left-handed pitcher Frank "Noodles" Hahn demonstrates his windup to a cameraman before a Reds game at Redland Field in the early 1900s.

When Hitting Became A Science
CY SEYMOUR

One of the oldest batting marks in the Cincinnati Reds record book is held by a player who started out as a pitcher.

Not even the hitting prowess of Pete Rose could match the one-season effort exhibited by James Bentley "Cy" Seymour in 1905. That season Seymour batted a robust .377 to lead all National League hitters and set a standard that remains unequaled today in the annals of the Reds.

Seymour was one of the most famous baseball players in the early 1900s. Four consecutive years after joining Cincinnati in 1902 from Baltimore, Seymour batted over .300. He was one of the most respected hitters of those infant days of baseball.

After winning the batting championship, Seymour was asked by a newspaper reporter in Cincinnati to explain why.

Seymour said, "If I were asked to give two principal suggestions for good batting, they would be: Know your pitcher and keep close tabs on the position of the fielders."

Today, the hit-and-run game is an important part of baseball, but when Seymour played, few batters were able to master the art. He was one who did.

"I ascribe a large portion of my showing last year to the hit-and-run game. I would give the runner on first base his signal to steal and then aim to hit the ball through the shortstop's or second baseman's position, according as the one or the other left it open to cover the bag and catch the runner," Cy said, after winning the league batting crown.

A standard practice in the early days of baseball was that many hitters would run to the front of the batter's box to hit the pitch before it curved. Seymour had his own theory which was to counter that practice.

"I rarely or never seek to run forward past the plate and meet the ball before the curve breaks," Seymour said. "By playing as far back of the plate as possible, I get that much more time to be sure which infielder is going to cover second base. A large portion of my base hits were made in this way."

Seymour was a scientific hitter. He even had different kinds of bats for different kinds of pitchers — highly unusual in an era when baseball was hardly as refined as it is today.

"I am not particular about using any special bat," Seymour said. "For a pitcher who serves slow ones and uses his head, I use a lighter bat; but when a pitcher relies mainly on speed I find a heavy bat more serviceable. I do not grasp the bat at the end because I find I can control it better and meet the ball more accurately by holding the bat a few inches from the end.... It is a mistake to try and slam the ball with all your might. Hit it a good solid lick, but you can do better inside work if you don't try to rip the cover off every time you swing at it."

Seymour started as a pitcher and won 25 games for the New York Giants in 1898. As often as not, however, he didn't have the slightest idea where his pitch might end up. He walked 213 batters in one season, enough to send him to the outfield. Fortunately, he could hit.

Noting his batting prowess, the Giants began working their left-hander occasionally into the lineup. Then, after Seymour joined John McGraw, the manager of the Baltimore club, in 1901, McGraw converted Seymour into a permanent outfielder.

After his arrival in the Reds camp, he was one of the most coveted players in baseball. Halfway through the 1906 season, Seymour was hitting only .257. That was 120 points less than his previous year's mark and the Reds sold their left fielder to the Giants.

The sale price was one of the highest of the day: $10,000. The

New York club was proud of the way it threw its cash around and it framed the canceled check and hung it in the team's offices.

While Seymour was a hard hitter, he was anything but a standout outfielder. While he had 13 assists one year to set a league record, any fly ball hit his way was an adventure. In 1908 he helped lose a playoff game for the Giants when he misjudged a long fly ball hit by Chicago's Joe Tinker. The ball wound up falling for a three-run triple. Had Seymour caught the ball, the Giants would have been league champions.

Seymour would be among today's millionaires playing baseball. But when he died in September of 1919 at the age of 46, six years after he quit playing, Seymour was penniless. Batting championships of 75 years ago just weren't worth much.

Cy Seymour set a Reds batting record in 1905 for the highest one-season average, .377, that still stands today.

A Pitching Trade That Backfired
CHRISTY MATHEWSON

Had the Reds not been looking for a veteran pitcher who might help them win the National League pennant in 1901, the great Christy Mathewson most likely would have done his pitching in Cincinnati rather than in New York.

During the 1900 season, the New York Giants had purchased the 19-year-old Mathewson from the Norfolk, Virginia, club; however, when he lost three games and was treated roughly by National League hitters, he was returned to the minor league team in Norfolk. The Reds then drafted him for only $100.

But manager Bid McPhee wanted a veteran pitcher, not the young and untested Mathewson, so he traded the young player away. McPhee went back to the Giants for Amos Rusie, a one-time star who won 243 games in his career, but who was finished by the time he came to the Reds.

The deal was a bomb, an atomic bomb. Rusie never won a game for the Reds. Mathewson went on to win 372 for the Giants, the third highest total in baseball history.

The first year after Mathewson was traded by the Reds, he won 20 games. He would go on to win at least 20 in 12 consecutive seasons, four times winning at least 30. The great debate of the era was: Who is the better pitcher? Christy Mathewson or Walter Johnson, the Washington Senators speedballer?

The Reds were Mathewson's favorite team. He picked on them relentlessly. In his career he won 64 games and lost only 18 to Cincinnati. In one stretch he beat Cincinnati 22 consecutive times, a National League record.

Mathewson eventually did pitch for the Reds, but by the time they got him, he was washed up, also.

In July 1916 manager Buck Herzog of the Reds was traded to the Giants. In return, the Reds received Bill McKechnie, Edd Roush and Mathewson, who was named the team's manager.

Matty figured on pitching some, too, but after one turn on the mound he retired. He won the game, his 373rd and final victory, but he gave up eight runs and immediately announced that he was retiring.

"I thought I could pitch a few more games," Mathewson said after beating the Cubs on September 4, 1916, "but I find that I haven't got the stuff anymore. I shall never attempt to pitch in a championship game again. If I ever go into the box again, I will buy every one of you a suit of clothes."

Christy never had to.

He remained solely the club's manager and moved the team up from seventh to fourth place in 1917 and had them in third in 1918 when he went into military action in World War I.

It was assumed after the Armistice that Mathewson would be back to skipper the 1919 Reds, but because club president Garry Herrmann couldn't reach his manager, Mathewson finally was replaced by Pat Moran who had been on the coaching staff of the New York Giants.

Ironically, when Mathewson returned home and found his job taken by Moran, Christy took Moran's vacated spot with the Giants under John McGraw.

Six years later one of the greatest pitchers in baseball history was dead. He had been gassed while in the service and had never fully recovered. In 1936, when the first five members of baseball's Hall of Fame were inducted, Christy Mathewson was one of them. That great record might have been accomplished as a Red, but . . .

Christy Mathewson, manager of the Reds in 1916, 1917 and 1918, tips his hat to the crowd at Redland Field. Before being named Reds manager, he was one of baseball's greatest pitchers.

The High Price Of A League War
SAM CRAWFORD

One of the most unfortunate events in Cincinnati Reds history was losing Sam Crawford to the Detroit Tigers. The Reds didn't trade him or sell his contract or even send him to the American League team via waivers. Instead, Crawford's contract was awarded to the Tigers to help settle the 1903 war between the well-established National League and the fledgling American League.

Crawford, a hard-hitting outfielder who was elected to baseball's Hall of Fame in 1957, played four seasons for Cincinnati, including 1901 when he hit the fantastic high number of 16 home runs. But after the 1902 season, Crawford signed two contracts, one with the Reds and another with Detroit, which was starting business in the American League.

About a dozen players signed two contracts and it looked like a player war would unfold, not dissimilar to the one that took place in the early 1960s when the American Football League and National Football League were engaged in bidding for collegiate football stars.

Crawford and pitcher Christy Mathewson of the New York Giants were the two most prominent players to sign two contracts. But before the two leagues became involved in an all-out war, peace was achieved. One of the conditions was that Crawford was awarded to the Tigers while Mathewson was returned to the Giants.

It was unfortunate for the Reds. Crawford would go on to become one of the all-time great hitters.

"His misfortune," Ty Cobb, a teammate of Crawford's at Detroit, said in 1955, "was that he played big league ball 50 years too early. If he were swinging away today, he'd be up with the all-time home run leaders."

Crawford is the only player to lead both leagues in home runs. His 16 topped the National League in 1901 and when he hit seven for Detroit in 1908, he also led that league. Home runs weren't easy in those days with a dead ball and Crawford knew that.

"Sometimes," he recalled shortly before his death in 1968, "we'd play a whole game with one ball, if it stayed in the park. Lopsided and black, and full of tobacco juice and licorice stains."

Crawford was a native of Wahoo, Nebraska. He loved that part of the country. On the day he was elected to the Hall of Fame, he told the museum's curator in Cooperstown, New York:

"When you make up my plaque have it read, 'Wahoo Sam.' That's my hometown and I'm proud of it."

Crawford, who was studying to be a barber when he decided to play baseball for a living, started his professional career in 1899 with Chatham, Ontario, in the Canadian League. He moved to Grand Rapids, Michigan, after only 43 games. Before that season was over, the Reds had purchased his contract. The first day Crawford saw a major league game, he got five hits, playing in a double-header when the Reds played the Cleveland Wanamakers in one game and Louisville in the other.

Crawford's major league career spanned 19 years and he had a .310 lifetime average. He missed 3,000 hits by only 36. Five times he led the American League in triples and his 312 three-base hits remains all-time No. 1.

Sam Crawford is the only player in baseball history to lead both the National and American League in home runs.

A Stolen Base That Was Found
BOB BESCHER

They aimed at his stolen-base record for half a century, but not until Maury Wills came along in 1962 did anyone steal more bases in one National League season than former Reds outfielder Bob Bescher.

Bescher rivaled the American League's legendary Ty Cobb on the base paths. He stole 81 in 1911 and that figure remained the National League standard until Wills passed him on his way to 104 some 51 years later.

Bescher's career with the Reds lasted six years — 1908 through 1913. Four times he led the National League in stolen bases.

He was one of the biggest players of his day, 6 feet and approximately 200 pounds. He wasn't a particularly good hitter, owning only a .258 lifetime batting average, but he could get on base. The year he stole 81 bases, he drew 102 walks. One other season he led the league with 94 walks.

He was noted for having a tremendous hook slide that helped him elude many tags at second base. In 1911 he was thrown out only three times in 84 attempts to steal.

Bescher was a switch-hitter who played left field and he was popular with the fans and press.

Jack Ryder, the long-time Cincinnati baseball writer, described Bescher after a double-header with St. Louis on June 1, 1911:

"The best feature of the team's play was the all-around performance of Mr. Robert Bescher, who shone at all angles. Bob got six hits and stole five bases in the two games besides fielding his position with a great deal of speed. He gave a better exhibition on sacks than anyone who has shown here for a long time."

Long before Knute Rockne was building a football institution at Notre Dame, the school was turning out athletes of prominence. One of them was Bob Bescher. He played the outfield on the Fighting Irish baseball team for three years.

Later, but before starting his professional baseball career in 1906, Bescher spent about a year on a Nebraska cattle ranch; then he returned to Ohio where he was a high-scoring running back on the football team for Wittenberg College in Springfield.

Bescher played baseball in Dayton for three years before he was sold to Cincinnati for $1,800 in September 1908. He made his debut on September 8. Before the end of that month, he had stolen 10 bases.

After Bescher left the Reds, he helped the New York Giants win the pennant in 1914, but he spent only one season with that club. He couldn't get along with the fiery New York manager, John McGraw.

Bescher went to St. Louis in 1915, and he finished up his career in 1918 with Cleveland.

One of the best ways to describe Bescher was hard-nosed. He never would avoid a fight. After being cursed by St. Louis manager Roger Bresnahan one day in Cincinnati, Bescher landed a haymaker to the mouth of the Cardinals skipper. According to newspaper accounts, Bresnahan spent the next morning at a Cincinnati dentist's office.

In the off-season, Bescher was an avid hunter. He was a native of London, Ohio, a small town in the central part of the state, and lived in his hometown after retirement and worked for years as an oil inspector for the state of Ohio. He died in 1942, killed when a train slammed into his car.

Hardly anyone is alive today from the Bob Bescher era. Even Edd Roush, the Hall-of-Famer who played in the teens and the twenties, recalls little about Bescher.

"I'm 87 and he played before my time," Roush said. "Heck, all of those fellows he played with are dead."

Bescher's name was brought back to life, though, in the summer of 1980 when Dave Collins challenged Bescher's Cincinnati base-stealing record. Collins fell two short.

Amid the hoopla and the instant research the record books have been changed. Since 1911, it was recorded that Bescher owned the Cincinnati record with 80 stolen bases. But one additional theft was found when Peter King, a young reporter with *The Cincinnati Enquirer,* went through the box scores of the 1911 season and came up with 81 steals. A base that Bescher stole on July 13 was never logged into the books.

King submitted the additional steal to baseball's Records Committee. After discussion and a look at King's evidence, Bescher was given another stolen base, some 70 years after the fact.

Outfielder Bob Bescher loosens up before a game at Redland Field in the early 1900s. Bescher still holds the Reds one-season stolen base record.

The Father Of The World Series
GARRY HERRMANN

August "Garry" Herrmann was president of the Cincinnati Reds for 25 years, but it was in his role as chairman of the national commission of baseball that Herrmann made his greatest impact on the game he so dearly loved.

Garry Herrmann was, in effect, baseball's first commissioner and, as commission chairman, he was chiefly responsible for the birth of the World Series.

Herrmann served on the commission with the presidents of the National and American leagues. He had the top voice in any ruling. In 1903 the Pittsburgh Pirates and the Boston Red Sox, the two leagues' champions, met in a post-season playoff. These games are generally regarded as the first World Series, but it was, in reality, simply an interclub affair. Nonetheless, it generated a lot of interest among baseball fans.

The following year, 1904, there was considerable disappointment among the fans when the champion New York Giants and Philadelphia Athletics failed to meet in a post-season series. After they failed to play, Herrmann took action.

Working with the two league presidents, he drew up an agreement and the commission enacted legislation for the first official World Series, in 1905.

Herrmann was given the nickname "Garry" by a foreman in the type foundry where he worked as a youngster in Cincinnati. He had been a baseball fan most of his life, but he didn't become active in the professional game officially until 1902 when political leader George B. Cox and the Fleischmann family purchased the Reds for about $150,000.

As a young man, Herrmann had discovered that the surest way to Cincinnati prominence was through ward politics. He worked his way up in the system and became one of the most influential politicians, running city hall for Cox. In August 1902, when Cox and the Fleischmanns purchased the Reds, they installed the 43-year-old Herrmann as the club's president. He remained at the post until October 10, 1927, when ill health — hardening of the arteries — sent him into retirement.

Herrmann served as president of the Reds and as chairman of the national commission until 1920 when the commission was dissolved and Judge Kennesaw Mountain Landis was appointed the commissioner of baseball. Landis' appointment followed the ill-fated 1919 World Series when eight members of the White Sox were accused of having "thrown" games to the Reds. The accusations were never proved.

Herrmann's happiest year, no doubt, was the 1919 season. The Reds had been reorganized, but he remained president. When the team appeared headed for bankruptcy, Herrmann found a way to keep the franchise afloat. He hired Pat Moran as the manager and the team won the city's first National League championship, and then won the World Series.

Two of Herrmann's fondest dreams were never fulfilled, though. He envisioned a permanent spring-training home for the Reds in Orlando, Florida, complete with a hotel, golf course and several baseball diamonds. The other dream was a new ballpark for Cincinnati.

Garry Herrmann was the life of any party he threw or attended and there were plenty of both.

"He was the living personification of Cincinnati culture," Lee Allen wrote in his book, *The Cincinnati Reds*. "To remember him is to remember the outdoor beer gardens and the vaudeville, the singing waiters, the foaming steins of beer, the Liederkrantz sandwiches, the belching, guffawing laughter of long forgotten nights."

Herrmann is said to be the man who was responsible for fried pigs' feet being added to the breakfast menu at New York's Waldorf-Astoria Hotel. He was a portly guy. He wore loud, checked clothes and often displayed diamond rings on both hands. His favorite food was sausage and he took it with him wherever he went. He traveled first-class. He always had an entourage. And he always paid the tab.

Garry Hermann was not only a baseball celebrity. He was well-known in other areas, too. When he worked at city hall, he was charged with constructing Cincinnati's waterworks. On its completion, it was considered the best in the world. Built for some $11 million, engineers estimated its value at more than $20 million a couple of years after it was constructed.

He liked bowling. In 1908 he was elected president of the American Bowling Congress. He brought the national bowling convention to Cincinnati and it ranked as the best ever by the organization.

He also was a member of the Cincinnati Elks Lodge. He led the Cincinnati chapter to the forefront of American Lodges and became the Grand Exalted Ruler of all Elks in America.

But more than anything else, Herrmann was a baseball man. The success of the World Series since its inception is just one more reason why Herrmann is remembered as one of the all-time great baseball executives.

Garry Herrmann, president of the Reds for 25 years, is called the father of the World Series because of his early input into the Fall Classic.

From A Flooded Field To The Flag
PAT MORAN

If the spring of 1919 had been an omen of things to come, the Cincinnati Reds would have finished last that year. Instead, they won the National League pennant.

It was probably the worst spring-training experience a Cincinnati team ever endured.

In some respects, the camp was doomed from the start. The Reds were broke. Only some last minute maneuvering by team president Garry Herrmann enabled the team to journey south.

The site picked was Waxahachie, Texas, a little town in the southern part of the state. When the Reds arrived in February, so did the monsoon season. It rained day after day. The ballpark was situated in one of the lowest parts of the city; consequently, the playing field constantly was flooded.

The Reds players got so desperate they ended up playing in the railroad yards, in a cemetery, in a cow pasture and in a lot next to the town's bus depot. Batting practice seldom was taken and infield practice was a figment of their imaginations. About all they could do was throw and run.

What made the situation worse was that Pat Moran was in his first year as the Reds manager. He had been hired to replace Christy Mathewson, who had been drafted in 1918 and was in Europe. When Mathewson didn't respond to Herrmann's cablegrams about returning to the helm of the Reds in 1919, Herrmann had no choice but to look for a new manager. Moran had led the Philadelphia Phillies to the National League pennant in 1915 and he was hired away from the New York Giants coaching staff.

When the Reds finally left Waxahachie for a barnstorming trip north, they encountered more rain and were able to play only a few exhibition games. The team was a shambles.

Edd Roush, Lee Magee and Jimmy Ring were holdouts and hadn't bothered to report to spring training. Other players, like Rube Bressler, were just returning from World War I.

But Moran persevered. When the Reds finally arrived home a few days before the regular season was to begin, things began falling into place. Roush came to Cincinnati, signed his contract and was ready to go by Opening Day. Pitcher Slim Sallee, who had back problems in Waxahachie, was set to go. A new second baseman, Maury Rath, played well above expectations.

Moran had a positive influence on the club. The team played with reckless abandon. They won their first seven games and went on that season to beat the New York Giants by nine games. It was the first pennant for Cincinnati, which had joined the National League as a charter member in 1876.

Much of the credit for the team's success went to Moran. He credited hard work for the team's success.

"The one real secret is work," Moran said in an interview after the 1919 season. "Baseball, just like everything else, is a business. You cannot succeed in business unless you work. The same principle applies to the national pastime."

The Reds never repeated as pennant-winners under Moran's managerial guidance, but they were always contenders. Moran remained the Cincinnati skipper until he died in March 1924, when the Reds were at work in Orlando, Florida. He was long a hard-living man who liked to drink, and it caught up with him. His death officially was listed as a result of Bright's disease, but many knew that his life style had taken its final toll.

Cincinnati manager Pat Moran (right) and pitcher Slim Sallee look over the crowd before a game at Redland Field. Moran piloted the Reds to a pennant his first year, 1919.

A Mean Bat And A Mean Negotiator
EDD ROUSH

There never may have been a major league baseball player tougher to sign than Edd Roush, the former Reds center fielder who is enshrined in baseball's Hall of Fame.

He always seemed to be a holdout, going to such an extreme one year that he sat out the entire season when he couldn't reach contract terms.

The 1922 season is a good example of Roush's stubbornness. The hard-hitting outfielder had batted a robust .352 in 1921 and he demanded a big raise. The Reds said no. So Roush decided he wouldn't report to spring training with the team in Mineral Wells, Texas. He stayed on his farm in Oakland City, Indiana.

Opening Day came and Roush remained on the farm. The Reds, sorely missing his explosive bat, struggled. The team won one of its first 12 games. Manager Pat Moran was getting desperate. He phoned Roush and asked him to sign. But Roush said, "No." He remained a holdout who wanted a higher salary.

May 1, 1922, was the day that it looked like Roush was finished with the Reds. Club president Garry Herrmann announced that Roush would not be welcome in Cincinnati.

"The Cincinnati ball club," Herrmann wrote in a statement issued to Cincinnati newspapers, "is definitely through with Edd Roush. We have decided not to ask him to return even on our terms, to say nothing of his. There is no place where he could really strengthen this club, as it is now made up, and he will be allowed to stay right where he is. This is the last word. Mr. Roush will not play with the Reds during the 1922 season."

Both parties, however, gave in. Herrmann accepted Roush back on the club and Roush agreed to sign under the Reds terms. Edd Roush returned on July 23 and played in 49 games. He hadn't had spring training, he had not played any ball in almost one year. But he still tore the cover off the baseball. He batted .352 again, an incredible testament to his batting skill.

"I never saw anyone like him," manager Moran once said. "All that fella has to do is wash his hands, adjust his cap and he's in shape to hit."

Roush was his own man, a ballplayer's ballplayer. He had a mind of his own and he often spoke it. It was because of his sharp tongue that he wound up with the Reds in 1916.

He was playing sparingly with the New York Giants and he wasn't happy. One afternoon Giants manager Jack McGraw questioned Roush's use of a 48-ounce bat, by far the heaviest of any used in baseball.

"Don't ever let me see you at the plate with that bat again," McGraw told Roush.

"This is the first damn league I ever played in," Roush snapped back to the man known as Little Napoleon, "where the manager picked your bat."

"What league did you ever hit .300 in?" McGraw challenged.

"I hit .300 in every league I was ever in, and I'd hit it in this one if you'd let me play regularly."

That was enough for McGraw. He couldn't get rid of Roush fast enough. He traded him to the Reds midway through the 1916 season. Edd batted .287 for the Reds that year. The following year, true to his words to McGraw, he hit .300.

Continued on page 50

In this 1923 photograph, Hall-of-Fame center fielder Edd Roush demonstrates to the cameraman how he caught fly ball after fly ball in his outfield position.

It wasn't exactly Rogue's Gallery, but Lee Magee, Pat Duncan, Edd Roush and Greasy Neale line up for this 1920 picture at Redland Field in Cincinnati.

Continued from page 48

In fact, he batted .341 and won the batting championship.

Roush played in Cincinnati from the summer of 1916 until 1927, when he was traded back to New York. As a regular with the Reds, he never failed to bat at least .300. In one stretch, he batted .339, .352, .352, .351, .348, and .339 in succession.

His defense was superb. There are some knowledgeable people who feel he might be the best defensive center fielder ever to play in baseball. Certainly, he ranks in the top five.

After the Reds traded him to New York, McGraw welcomed back his former bad boy with open arms and even offered Roush a three-year contract calling for $70,000, quite a sum in 1927. Roush readily accepted.

Center fielder Edd Roush, a member of baseball's Hall of Fame, takes batting practice before a game in the 1920s at Redland Field.

But Roush had one last contract squabble, and it was a big one. After batting .324 in 1929, Roush wanted a $15,000 raise. The Giants refused, so Roush went back to his farm in Indiana. This time he sat out the entire year, the only time in baseball history when a player held out the whole season over a salary dispute.

The Reds got permission to talk with Roush in the winter of 1930 and they struck a deal in which he would return to Cincinnati.

At the age of 38, after sitting out the previous season, Edd Roush came back to baseball. He played in 101 games and batted .271, an unbelievable figure at his age.

Today, Roush is the oldest living Hall-of-Famer at age 88. He remains as feisty and as outspoken as ever. He was one of the best. It's doubtful there ever will be another like him.

The Pitching "Virginia Gentleman" EPPA RIXEY

When Warren Spahn, the great Milwaukee Braves pitcher, won his 267th game in 1959, he set a record for most career victories by a left-handed pitcher.

The record was ballyhooed far and wide, and rightly so. But 26 years earlier when Eppa Rixey concluded his career with the Cincinnati Reds, retiring with 266 victories, this achievement virtually went unnoticed.

"Nobody even knew I had a record," Rixey said in a 1959 interview with the Newspaper Enterprise Association. "There wasn't so much emphasis in those days. Tom Swope, the baseball writer for *The Cincinnati Post*, gave me a copy of my record when I quit. He wrote that it was the best ever made in the league by a left-hander. It didn't rate national headlines."

Rixey was the kind of pitcher who didn't get many headlines, but in a 21-year career, 13 with the Reds, he certainly was one of baseball's best pitchers.

Four times he won at least 20 games, and in 1922 he had the most victories in the National League: 25.

Rixey never pitched an inning of minor league baseball, coming straight from the University of Virginia to the Philadelphia Phillies in 1912. He might be the only player ever scouted and signed by an umpire. Cy Rigler, coaching at Virginia at the time, was a Phillies scout and a National League umpire as well. He saw the 6-foot-5-inch left-hander's potential and got his signature on a Phillies contract.

Pitching until he was 43 years old, Rixey was well-known for being one of baseball's "best gentlemen." He always stayed in top physical condition and his delightful sense of humor made him a big favorite among his teammates.

Rixey's given name was Eppa Rixey Jr., but not long after he began playing with the Phillies, he acquired the middle name of Jeptha.

"The third game I won in the National League was in 1912 in Cincinnati. Bill Phelon, sports editor of *The Cincinnati Times Star*, had a flair for poems. He wrote one about me. My name didn't fill out the last line the way he wanted it, so he added to it. He called me 'Eppa Jeptha Rixey.'

"That isn't my name," Rixey emphasized, "my name is Eppa Rixey Jr. and that's all. But the Jeptha was picked up. People assumed it was right. I've got cousins in Virginia who write me that way. They believe it's my real name. Some of the record books carry it that way."

After Rixey retired, he waited for years for induction into baseball's Hall of Fame. Often mentioned as a possible Hall-of-Famer, the honor eluded him year after year. One summer, while on vacation, Rixey visited the Hall of Fame in Cooperstown, New York, and sent post cards to friends and business associates in Cincinnati.

"I finally made it to Cooperstown — for one day," he wrote.

Finally, however, his call came. On January 27, 1968, the Old-Timers Committee recognized Rixey for his great pitching and voted him into the Hall of Fame.

Unfortunately, though, he never lived to see his Hall of Fame plaque. One month after election, he died suddenly of a heart attack in Cincinnati.

Today Eppa Rixey is remembered as one of baseball's great left-handers and he remains the winningest pitcher in Cincinnati Reds history.

Hall-of-Fame left-hander Eppa Rixey won more games in a Cincinnati uniform than any pitcher in Reds history, 173. He was elected to the Hall of Fame in 1968.

A Latin Temper On The Mound
ADOLFO LUQUE

Before Fidel Castro and his Communist regime shut off the supply line in the early 1960s, Cuba sent a steady stream of players to baseball's major leagues.

One of the best was Adolfo Luque, a right-handed pitcher who spent 11½ years with the Cincinnati Reds. Luque joined Cincinnati after being purchased from the Louisville minor league club midway through the 1918 season.

In the following 11 years, he won 154 games.

Known as the elder statesman of Cuban baseball, Luque first came to the United States in 1912, imported by Dr. Hernandez Henriquez who owned the Long Branch, New Jersey, team of the New Jersey-York League. It was while he was with the Long Branch team that Luque was spotted as a hotshot pitcher.

Major league baseball, during this era, was not played in New York City on Sundays. To help pay their travel expenses to New York, visiting major league teams would play exhibition games on Sundays against the Long Branch team. The money came easy. The victories did not.

The major leagues had to contend with Luque and he beat them with regularity. George Stallings was manager of the 1914 Boston Braves, the team known as the Miracle Braves because of their rise from last place on July 4 to the National League pennant. He was so impressed with the Cuban's pitching that he signed Luque late in the 1914 season.

The strapping Cuban pitched in seven games that year and in only three the following year before he was shipped off to the minor leagues.

He wound up in Louisville in 1918. After he won 11 of his first 13 games, the Reds purchased Luque from the Louisville Colonels. It was to be one of the best buys the Reds ever made.

The Reds won their first National League championship in 1919 and Luque played a major role. Pitching in a relief role, he won 10 games and lost only three and then he worked five scoreless innings in two World Series appearances. Dolf Luque was well on his way to becoming a Reds standout.

In 1923 he had the best one-season performance in club history. He won 27 games, lost only eight and posted an earned run average of 1.93. Although Bucky Walters would later tie his 27 victories in 1939, that number stands today as the most games ever won in one year by a Reds pitcher.

Luque was a tough man and wouldn't give in to the hitter. Few ever dared to crowd the plate. When he hit a batter, it was on purpose.

Luque's temper was as fierce as his fastball. He had fights on the field, in the dugouts and in the clubhouse. One of his most famous confrontations came in Cincinnati when the Reds were playing the New York Giants.

There was an overflow crowd at Redland Field, Cincinnati's home park which later would be called Crosley Field. Because of the large crowd, fans were allowed to stand on the field and the player benches were moved out in front of the dugouts. The bench jockeys didn't even have to yell to get Luque's attention that afternoon.

Bill Cunningham, a reserve outfielder, was riding Luque the toughest that day. Ross Young was at bat when Luque decided he couldn't take Cunningham's insults anymore. Dolf put his glove on the pitching mound, ran to the Giants bench and took a mighty swing at Cunningham.

But Cunningham ducked. The man who was decked by Luque's flying fist was Casey Stengel — the same Charles Dillon "Casey" Stengel who became the famous Yankee manager.

A free-for-all ensued. When the umpires finally restored order, Luque was ejected from the game. But a moment later Luque was back on the field. This time he had a bat and was heading for the Giants bench. Four policemen intervened and led a struggling Luque from the field.

In February 1930, just before spring training, Luque was sold to Brooklyn. He pitched two seasons for the Dodgers and went to the Giants in 1932. He worked four seasons for them and, finally at the age of 45, retired as a player to become a New York coach.

Luque went back to his native Cuba where he was a legend, known by everyone. He died in July of 1957, prompting *New York Journal American* sportswriter Frank Graham to eulogize:

"It's hard to believe. Adolfo Luque was much too strong, too tough, too determined to die at this age of 66 . . . he died of a heart attack. Did he? It sounds absurd. Luque's heart failed him in the clutch? It never did before. How many close ball games did he pitch? How many did he win . . . or lose? When he won, it was sometimes on his heart. When he lost, it was never because his heart had missed a beat. Some enemy hitter got lucky or some idiot playing behind Luque fumbled a ground ball or dropped a sinking liner or was out of position so that he did not make the catch that should have been so easy for him."

Right-hander Dolf Luque was one of the best pitchers in Reds history. Here he works out at Redland Field. He was a 27-game winner in 1923.

Lights Out For The Shine Ball
HOD ELLER

When baseball outlawed the "shine ball" in 1920, no pitcher was hurt more than Cincinnati right-hander Horace "Hod" Eller who had helped the Reds to the National League pennant in 1919.

Eller's favorite "out" pitch was the "shine ball." In 1919 when he was 20-9 with a 2.39 earned run average, the "shine" was the talk of the country.

Eller worked long and hard on perfecting the delivery and had his own special way of throwing it. He rubbed the cover of the baseball with talcum powder, creating the unnatural and very slick surface. When delivered properly, the pitch did unbelievable things on its path to the plate. The ball might dip sharply at the last second. It might dart inside or out, confusing the batter. Or it might hop upward. It acted much like today's knuckle ball except that it was delivered with the speed and the motion of a fastball.

After the 1919 season, baseball's rules-makers decided the pitch was unfair and they declared it to be illegal. Eller, his best pitch outlawed, appealed to the president of the National League. His appeal went unanswered and in 1920 Eller had to resort to conventional weapons — fastball, curve or changeup.

His record dipped to 13-12 in 1920. The next year Eller pitched his last games in the major leagues. In addition to losing his best pitch, Eller began having arm problems. When he had a 2-2 record after 13 appearances, Eller was traded to Oakland of the Pacific Coast League. The Reds needed a third baseman and they came up with Babe Pinelli in exchange for the pitcher.

Eller originally might have made it to the major leagues with the Chicago White Sox, but that American League team wanted to pay only $1,500 to Moline of the Three I League for Eller's contract. Moline was asking $2,500. After training with the White Sox during the spring of 1916, Eller was returned to Moline. He encountered contract problems and the result was that he got his biggest break.

Eller joined a semipro team in Henryville, Illinois. Late in the season, the team played an exhibition game against Cincinnati. Eller pitched so well that Reds manager Christy Mathewson drafted Eller for the 1917 season.

Eller came back to haunt the White Sox during the 1919 World Series. He pitched the Reds to two victories, one a three-hit shutout, and he set a World Series record that still stands — fanning six consecutive batters. His victory in Game No. 8 clinched Cincinnati's first World Championship.

After the Reds sent Eller to Oakland in 1921, he played in the minors until 1925 when he retired. He returned to Indianapolis where he was a member of the police force for 22 years. He died in 1961.

One has to wonder how Eller's career might have prospered had the "shine ball" not been outlawed.

Hod Eller was a hero for the 1919 Reds when he threw his "shine ball" to perfection.

Quick Hands And Temper At Third
BABE PINELLI

His name was Rinaldo Angelo Paolinelli. He is best remembered for when he threw up his right hand and called Dale Mitchell out on strikes to bring to a close Don Larsen's perfect game in the 1956 World Series.

But this man, who changed his name to Ralph Pinelli, also was a better-than-average third baseman for the Cincinnati Reds.

It was a long and tough road for Pinelli to the major leagues. His father was killed in the 1906 San Francisco earthquake and Pinelli quit school at an early age to help provide for his family. His nickname "Babe" was given to him because he was the youngest — "the baby" — of his childhood group of friends.

He was quick with his hands and his temper and he seemed constantly embroiled in a fight. At one time he considered becoming a professional boxer after battering a promoter one evening in a bloody fight.

But baseball was his game. He first played professionally in 1917 with Portland in the Pacific Coast League. He briefly made it to the majors with the Chicago White Sox in 1918, but the following year he was back with Sacramento in the PCL. That season almost ended Babe's baseball career forever.

He had a clubhouse fight with his manager, Bill Rogers, who fined Pinelli $50 for sitting on the bench with a sprained ankle instead of resting at the hotel. Later that year Pinelli decked an umpire, one of the most serious offenses a player can commit.

Home plate umpire Bill Byron called a strike on Pinelli and the two engaged in a wild argument. Byron accidently bumped into Pinelli, hitting him with his mask. That sent Pinelli into a frenzy and he punched the umpire, knocking him down.

"I should have known that it was an accident, that Byron didn't mean to strike me with that mask, but I simply lost control of myself," Pinelli said in a *Sporting News* interview in 1956 just after he retired himself as an umpire.

Al Jolson, the great singer, was in the stands that afternoon and later came to Pinelli's defense. He sent a telegram to league president William McCarthy explaining the situation. Finally, with Pinelli sweating out the decision, McCarthy simply slapped the young player's hands and cautioned him about fighting. The episode seemed to turn things around for Pinelli.

In 1920 Pinelli was back in the major leagues but batted only .229, and in 1921 he returned to the Pacific Coast League. It was at Oakland that he learned to be a hitter.

Outfielder Denny Wilie, who had played portions of three years in the major leagues in the early teens, took Pinelli under his wing.

"The first thing he did was put a golf club in my hand — a driver," Pinelli recalled. "He had me swing it to get the feel of following through. I had never realized what follow-through meant.

"After he was satisfied with my follow-through, he gave me a 40-ounce bat to swing. He told me the 40-ounce bat would teach me to learn to time the ball. With the big bat I no longer would try to kill the ball. Instead, I would master control of the bat with good timing.

"His instructions must have been right, because that year I had the greatest batting success I ever enjoyed."

Pinelli hit .339 for Oakland and the Reds came calling, checkbook in hand. The Reds paid Oakland $35,000 for Pinelli and sent three players to the PCL club to boot.

When Pinelli arrived in Cincinnati, he found himself in familiar surroundings. He was playing on an all-San Francisco infield. Lew Fonseca was at first base, Sammy Bohne was at second, Jimmy Caveney was at short and Pinelli was at third.

"I'll bet," Pinelli said, "it's the only time in major league history

After retiring as a player, Babe Pinelli turned to umpiring. He was behind the plate at the first night game at Crosley Field, in 1935, and called Don Larsen's perfect World Series game in 1956.

an entire infield was from the same town."

Pinelli remained hot-tempered with the Reds but was ejected from only one game.

One argument had the Reds clubhouse rocking with laughter. It involved Dolph Luque, the Cuban pitcher, and Pinelli. One day after Pinelli made a suggestion to Luque on how to pitch a certain batter, Luque went into a rage. He grabbed a pair of scissors and stormed after the third baseman. Bohne intercepted Luque and grabbed the weapon, but Luque wasn't finished.

"You get taxicab, I get taxicab, then we get guns and have a duel," said a deadly serious Luque. The rest of the team howled with laughter, taking the heat out of the situation. The incident blew over and the two became good friends.

"He was a nice fellow most of the time," Pinelli said of Luque. "He just happened to have a temper that was even worse than mine."

Pinelli's career with the Reds ended in 1927 and he returned to play in the Pacific Coast League through the 1932 season. By then, he had decided to become an umpire.

Odds were 10 to 1 against his success because of his fighting record, but he succeeded. Not only did he become a good umpire, he became a great one.

He was the home plate umpire in Cincinnati when the first night game was played at Crosley Field. His swan song was Larsen's perfect game against Brooklyn in the 1956 World Series.

It was quite a way, indeed, to end a career, calling "Strike three" on the final out of the only perfect game in World Series history.

From College To Pros And Back
ETHAN ALLEN

One of the relatively few early-era baseball players to jump straight from the college campus to major league baseball was Ethan Allen. Allen, after his days as a Cincinnati Reds outfielder, gained fame as baseball coach for Yale's Elis.

The year was 1926, Allen's senior year at the University of Cincinnati. He had established himself as a standout in baseball, basketball and track for the Bearcats. It would be the season he went from the college sandlot to Redland Field, the name of Cincinnati's home field in the 1920s.

"The Reds offered me a bonus of $3,500 to sign, plus $5,000 more if I made the team," Allen recalled in an interview in the Chapel Hill (N.C.) newspaper.

"Actually they could have had me for $2,500 the year before if they'd been willing to put that sum up, but they declined to go any higher than $1,500.

"Then Detroit and Cleveland got interested in me, and I spent a week on the road with the Indians under Tris Speaker, and three days in Detroit with Ty Cobb. The upshot was that Detroit offered me $8,500 to sign with them, and the Reds had to match that offer."

Allen spent most of that first season sitting on Cincinnati's bench, playing in only 18 games. From there he went on to join the select circle of lifetime .300 hitters, batting an even .300 in his career that ended in 1938 when he was released by the St. Louis Browns.

Allen was always interested in the scientific approach to baseball. The result was his first book on the game in 1938 entitled *Baseball Play and Strategy.*

"When I came up there was little teaching of the fundamentals done," Allen said.

"You were supposed to pick up everything on your own. I wanted to do something that would make it easier for young players to learn the fundamentals of the game."

At the same time, Allen developed an interest in movies and, when he was released by the Browns, he began to produce baseball movies for the National League.

In 1941 Allen marketed his own baseball game for kids called "All-Star Baseball." A second, more advanced game, "Strategic All-Star Baseball," came out in 1969.

"When I first introduced the game back in 1941," Allen recalled, "I had no trouble getting permission from various big league players to use disks with their records and skills. But nowadays the players have agents and so forth, and some want to be paid for having their records used. You'd think they would have wisdom enough to see that the publicity was worth more to them in the long run."

Allen played for the Reds only three full seasons. After a slow start in 1930, he was traded to John McGraw's New York Giants. He spent two years there and went to the Cardinals. From there, it was on to Philadelphia the next year. He was with the Cubs in 1936 and finished out his career with St. Louis in 1938.

In 1946 he succeeded Red Rolfe, the old New York Yankees third baseman, as coach at Yale and was acknowledged as one of the top college coaches in the business. His Yale teams won five conference championships and twice were finalists in the National Collegiate Athletic Association college world series. Vice President George Bush was a first baseman on those two teams.

He is now retired and living in Chapel Hill, North Carolina, a town he fell in love with while a college coach.

Allen remains a favorite with the game-playing set. His "All-Star Baseball" game is produced by Cadaco, Inc., and Allen frequently receives letters from the game-playing hobbyists who write with suggestions and queries.

"People sometimes ask me whether I like being out of baseball," Allen added. "I'm not out of it. It's been my life work, and I'm just as involved in it as ever, and I hope to keep right on being involved for the rest of my life."

Outfielder Ethan Allen went from the University of Cincinnati campus to the Cincinnati Reds and then returned to the college scene as the baseball coach at Yale.

The Long Wait Behind The Plate
BUBBLES HARGRAVE

Eugene "Bubbles" Hargrave is the perfect example of a baseball player who wouldn't give up. Way down deep, he knew he'd make it some day. Indeed, he did make it — as a great catcher with the Cincinnati Reds.

Starting a professional baseball career at the age of 19, Hargrave didn't make it to the major leagues for good until 11 years later. Following that, at the age of 34 when most catchers are ready to do something else, he won the National League batting title.

It was the first time in the modern era of baseball that a catcher had won a hitting crown. Since Hargrave, only one other catcher has equaled that feat — the Reds Ernie Lombardi.

Hargrave began his career in Terre Haute, Indiana, in 1911. Two years later the Chicago Cubs signed him to a major league contract. He caught very little and batted even less, so the Cubs sent him to the Class AA Kansas City team. After two years there, Hargrave was sent deeper into the minor leagues, landing at Memphis in the Class A Southern League.

He was 26 years old by then, but he wouldn't give up. The following year, 1919, Hargrave went to St. Paul, Minnesota. Suddenly he began hitting. Major league clubs took notice and, after the 1920 season, the Reds plunked down $10,000 and purchased Hargrave from the St. Paul team.

Bubbles batted .289 his first season in Cincinnati. Six straight years after that, though, he hit at least .300 and established himself as one of baseball's premier catchers.

He was the perfect backstop. He had sturdy legs, a strong arm and a cool head. Few base runners dared run on him. For good reason, too. In 1923 he threw out 90 would-be stealers.

To win the batting championship in 1926, Hargrave had to beat the great Rogers Hornsby, who had won it six straight years. Hornsby slumped badly to .317 and Hargrave wasn't challenged, except by teammate Rube Bressler. Bressler actually batted higher for the season, .357 to .353, but since he didn't play in at least 100 games, he wasn't eligible for the batting title.

Hargrave credited a spring sickness with his big year. He had an attack of appendicitis during spring training, but he refused to allow his appendix to be removed. Instead, he went on a strict diet and lost 14 pounds.

He got off to a great start and enjoyed the best year of his life.

Hargrave ended his baseball career in the early 1930s and settled in Cincinnati where he was a supervisor at a valve company. He kept a close eye on baseball and didn't like some of the things he saw.

"There's too much delay — too much changing of pitchers and running out to the mound every time a pitcher gets in a jam," Hargrave said in an Associated Press interview in 1956. "I'd stop all consultation between pitcher and manager out on the rubber.

"When we were going to make a change, the manager announced to the umpire who was coming in to pitch and that was it, except for a short session between the pitcher and the catcher to make sure of the signs.

"In my years under Pat Moran (the manager) he would ask me about a pitcher with 'How is he?' If I replied, 'Not so hot,' he'd just pitch somebody else."

Catcher Bubbles Hargrave (right) goes over the signals with pitcher Eppa Rixey before an old-timers game at Crosley Field. Hargrave won the 1926 batting championship.

The Two Who Shared Left Field
BRESSLER/CHRISTENSEN

Bubbles Hargrave wasn't the only .350 hitter on the 1926 Reds. In fact, two of his teammates hit higher than Hargrave's .353.

Raymond "Rube" Bressler and Walter "Cookoo" Christensen had good seasons, too. Bressler hit four points higher than Hargrave's league-leading .353 mark, but couldn't win the batting title because he appeared in only 86 games. League rules at that time stated a player had to play in at least 100 games to be eligible for the batting championship. Christensen batted an even .350, missing the batting title by only three points.

Both players are interesting characters.

Bressler grew up in Pennsylvania, moving from town to town with his family. His father was a lumberjack, and when the trees were stripped, they'd move elsewhere. In fact, Bressler's birthplace — Coder, Pennsylvania — no longer exists. It was only a temporary village constructed by the lumber company.

Bressler eventually wound up in Renova, Pennsylvania, where he was discovered as a baseball player. The Philadelphia Athletics signed him. At the age of 20, he was playing in a World Series, not as a hitter but as a pitcher. Bressler had played a great role in Philadelphia's drive to the American League title. He won 10 games, lost only three and posted a glittering 1.77 earned run average.

His major league career as a pitcher, however, was relatively short-lived. He lost 17 games in his second season in Philadelphia and was shuffled off to Atlanta in the minor leagues. He regained his touch there, winning 25 games, and the Reds purchased him in 1917. Rube won eight games in 1918 and pitched some in 1919, but his greatest contribution to the World Champion Reds came when he was switched to the outfield.

First baseman Jake Daubert had an idea and advanced it to manager Pat Moran. It was Daubert's notion that Bressler swung the bat well enough to be a regular outfielder. The Reds, needing a left fielder, decided to take a shot. The results were magnificent.

Bressler wound up playing 61 games in the outfield in 1919 and batted .306. Except for a few games on the mound the next year, Bressler remained an outfielder. No telling how good he might have become had he not broken his ankle in 1920. That slowed him down.

Not many hitters batted like Bressler. First, he was a left-handed thrower and a right-handed batter. That is highly unusual. Second, he hit from a deep crouch, uncoiling as the pitch sped plateward. Bressler was a line-drive hitter with little power. His 19-year career produced only 32 home runs, but he did finish with a .301 average.

Bressler's teammate for two years in Cincinnati was Cookoo Christensen. He played for Cincinnati in 1926 and 1927, the only two years he was in the major leagues.

The Reds purchased him from St. Paul of the American Association and it seemed that everything Christensen connected with in his first year was a hit. Bloops fell just between the infielders and outfielders. Line drives just managed to elude the outstretched arms of the shortstop and second baseman. Slowly hit balls on the infield became "leg" hits. It was certainly Christensen's year. Had there been a Rookie of the Year Award in those days, he would have won hands down.

Christensen was a left-handed hitter and was platooned in left field with Bressler. He delighted the crowds with his clowning. When he would make a catch that was a bit tougher than normal, Christensen would often turn a flip as the crowd cheered. He was a bench jockey, too, always baiting the umpires and opposing players. He was a hot-dog in the purest sense.

But Christensen didn't last long. He played in only 57 games in 1927 and then faded into oblivion, drifting off like so many of those one-season hotshots whom baseball has seen through the ages.

Rube Bressler was a pitcher-turned-outfielder who played a big role in the success of the Reds in the early 1920s.

The Great Pinch-Hitting Pitcher RED LUCAS

As strange as it sounds, one of the greatest pinch hitters in baseball history was a pitcher.

The pitcher with the penchant for coming off the bench with timely hits was Charles Fred Lucas, better known as "Red" Lucas when he played in Cincinnati from 1926 through 1933.

In a big league career that spanned the years from 1923 through 1938, Lucas accumulated 114 pinch-hits and set a record that stood until Smoky Burgess, who once played for the Reds, set a new standard in 1965.

Four different times in his career, Lucas led the National League in most pinch-hits in a season. He collected a personal high of 15 in 1930 when he appeared in 68 games in a pinch-hitting role.

Lucas was such an effective pinch hitter that it was easy to overlook the fact that he also was a standout pitcher. He often was called lucky because his defense seemed to make one remarkable play after another behind him, but Lucas defended his pitching.

"I guess the object of the game is to get the opposition out," he told baseball historian Lee Allen. "A lot of batters said they enjoyed hitting against me — I know Bill Terry was one of them — but the batter who gave me the most trouble was Blimp Phelps of the Dodgers. During the eight years I pitched for the Reds, we finished in the first division only once, but I usually managed to win more games than I lost."

An appreciation of Lucas' effectiveness as a Cincinnati pitcher can be gained by checking the Reds position in the standings during his career. During his eight years, the Reds were last three times, finished seventh twice, fifth twice and second once. Nevertheless, he won 109 games and lost 99 during that stretch.

A part-time relief pitcher and part-time starter during his first three years with the Reds, Lucas moved into the starting rotation permanently in 1929, except for five relief appearances in 1930.

Although he never won 20 games, Lucas came close several times. His best year was 1929 when he was 19-12. Undoubtedly Lucas would have won 20 on several occasions had he been pitching for a stronger team.

He was a workhorse. In 1929 he pitched 28 complete games, the most in the league. He again led the National League in complete games in 1931 and 1932. It was during those two seasons he established a Reds record that will probably never be broken.

Between August 13, 1931, and July 15, 1932, Lucas pitched 250 consecutive innings without being relieved. Today, a streak like that is unheard of. It was remarkable back in those days, too, but the Reds bullpen was so spotty, a tired Lucas often was better than anyone coming to his aid.

Lucas originally was signed by the New York Giants. He was only 5 feet 9 inches tall, and New York manager John McGraw thought Lucas was too small to become a big-time pitcher. The following year Lucas was shipped to the Boston Braves.

Because of his strong bat, Boston manager Dave Bancroft believed he had a second baseman and in the spring of 1925 Lucas was made an infielder. He played only six games with the Braves and was sent to the Seattle club of the Pacific Coast League because Boston owed that minor league team a player from an earlier deal.

Lucas had a 9-5 record and a 2.82 earned run average with Seattle and he became a hot property for the minor league team. Seattle president Charles Lockard sent a letter to Reds president Garry Herrmann offering Lucas to the Reds.

". . . is one of the sensations of the Pacific Coast League," the letter said in part. "Not only is he a good pitcher having won five and lost one to date, but also (is) an in(fielder) or outfielder. He is known as the Frank Merriwell of this league having a batting average of over 500 percent in games participated in. Only last week he went to bat as a pinch hitter on three different occasions against San Francisco and hit a home run on each trip, one with the bases loaded and again with two men on. He is a great hustler and will make good on any major league club...."

The Reds sent a scout to look at Lucas. When the season was over, the Reds worked out a deal with the Seattle team.

Lucas played in Cincinnati, beginning in 1926, for eight years. In 1933, he was dealt to the Pittsburgh Pirates for Adam Comorosky. Lucas finished up his major league career after the 1938 campaign, but not until he made the Reds regret they had ever peddled him. He beat Cincinnati 14 straight times as a member of the Pirates.

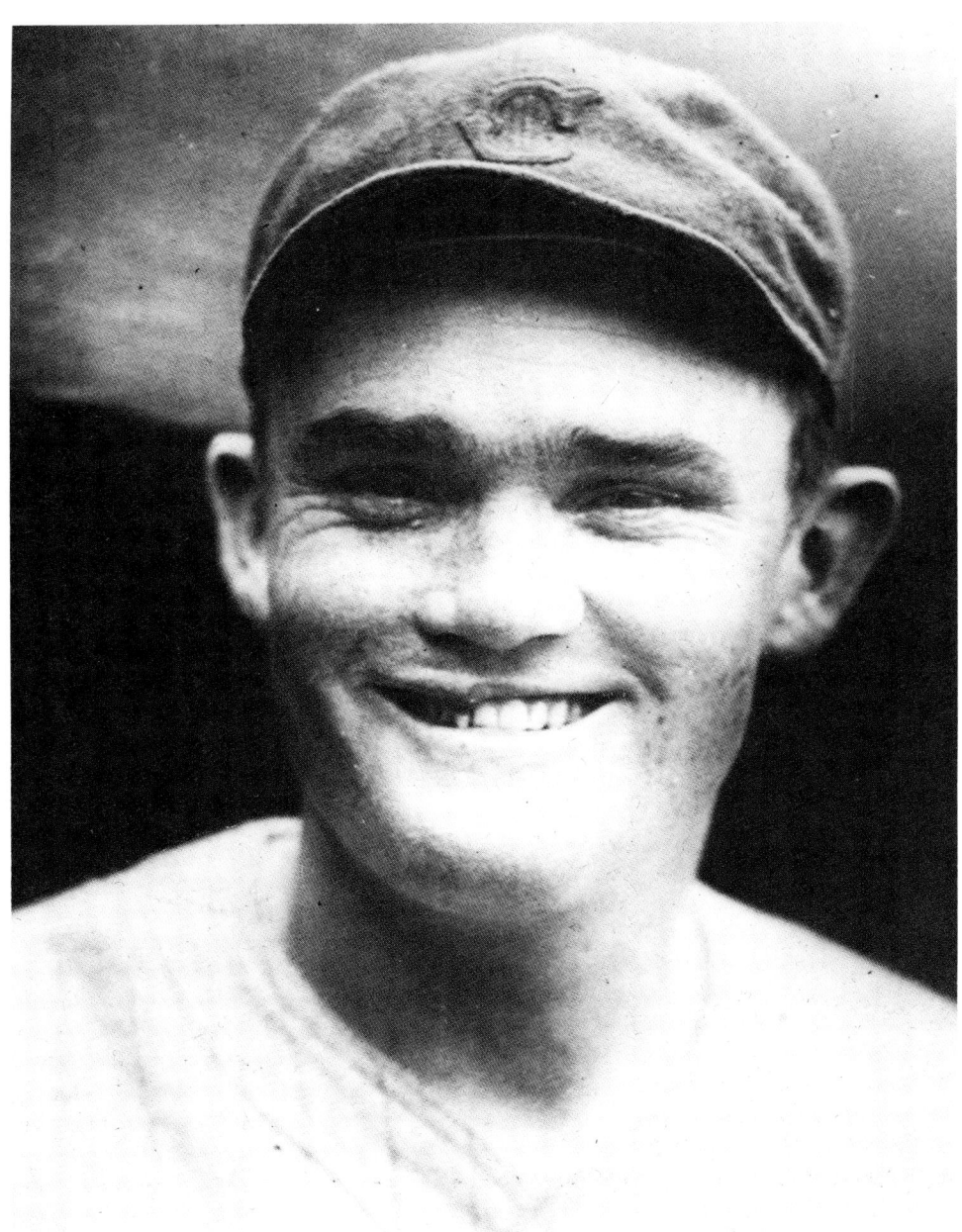

Charles "Red" Lucas was one of the best-hitting pitchers ever to play baseball. This 1926 photo captured his usual broad smile.

Who Turned On The Lights?
LARRY MacPHAIL

Loud Larry. The Barnum of baseball. Feisty. Impetuous. Those were just some of the words used to describe one-time Cincinnati Reds general manager Leland Stanford MacPhail, simply known as Larry MacPhail, baseball executive.

MacPhail was one of the first to use razzle-dazzle to entice baseball fans to the ballpark. He was the father of night baseball. He originated the stadium club idea at the ballpark. He was the first general manager to put his team into the air for all its road-game travel.

MacPhail reported to Cincinnati on November 7, 1933, as the Reds general manager. "He was 43 years old, dressed immaculately in various shades of tan and gray, and crowned by a hat with the brim invariably turned down," baseball historian Lee Allen wrote in his book, *The Cincinnati Reds*.

One of MacPhail's first jobs was to convince Powel Crosley, the Cincinnati automobile and radio tycoon, to purchase the Reds. MacPhail did a magnificent job and Crosley bought controlling interest in February 1934.

Next MacPhail began putting together a farm system for Cincinnati. He patterned the system after the St. Louis Cardinals, hiring popular Cincinnati sports figure Frank Lane to run it. Before MacPhail's first year had been completed, the Reds either owned outright or had working agreements with six farm clubs and they began developing their own players instead of relying on trades or contract purchases to stock the team.

In 1935 MacPhail convinced Crosley and other National League owners that night baseball was a necessity for the Reds to survive. He made his point and soon light standards were being erected in many other stadiums.

This man with wild and crazy ideas was at it again in 1936: he sent the Reds to San Juan, Puerto Rico, for part of their spring training.

MacPhail was ofttimes a hot-tempered individual and he could be hard to live with, especially if decisions didn't go his way. It was general knowledge that MacPhail and Crosley didn't always agree, but hardly anyone expected the announcement out of the Reds office on September 18, 1937: MacPhail had resigned.

When he left Cincinnati that autumn, MacPhail thought he was finished with baseball. He went to Michigan and joined his brother in the investment business. But he didn't stay there long. He wound up in Brooklyn as general manager of the Dodgers. Under MacPhail's direction, Brooklyn got out of debt. By the time he left for military service in World War II, the Dodgers had won their first pennant in 21 years.

After the war, MacPhail returned to baseball, this time with the New York Yankees. He and a pair of young millionaires, Del Webb and Dan Topping, bought the New York Yankees for $2.8 million. It was with the Yankees that he introduced the posh stadium club, an exclusive party room for the Yankees best customers. Yankee attendance rose by more than one million and he clearly was recognized as a great baseball executive.

He left baseball after the 1947 season and spent much of his later years in life with his second love, horse racing. He had a fine stable of horses in Maryland.

MacPhail passed on his love for sports to his sons. Lee MacPhail is president of the American League and William is a former vice president of CBS sports.

MacPhail died in 1975 but will be remembered eternally as the father of night baseball.

Larry MacPhail, called by some the Barnum of Baseball, was the father of night baseball in the major leagues, putting baseball under the lights in Cincinnati in 1935.

When Babe Was Almost A Player
HARRY STEVENS

If a certain baseball scout for the Cincinnati Reds had made a different choice one afternoon in Baltimore, Babe Ruth very well might have begun his major league baseball career in Cincinnati instead of Boston.

In 1914 the Reds had a "working agreement" with the Baltimore team, which played in the Class AAA International League. That agreement gave the Reds the right to pick two players from the Baltimore roster and sign them to a Cincinnati contract.

During the summer of 1914, Reds president Garry Herrmann sent his emissary to the East Coast to take a look at the Baltimore team. The man Herrmann selected was Harry Stevens. Stevens had no baseball experience; he was working for the Reds because he was a friend of the Fleischmann family, owners of the club.

Stevens was regarded by some as the proverbial company spy. A year earlier, 1913, he had ruffled some feathers when he joined the organization. Joe Tinker, manager of the Reds, took it as a personal insult that the club would hire a man to look after the players both at home and on the road, so he quit. The team hired Buck Herzog, who came from the New York Giants in a trade for outfielder Bob Bescher.

Other than his trips with the Reds in 1913, Stevens' baseball experience was minimal. Nevertheless, when the time came for a scout to be sent to Baltimore to look over the prospects, it was Stevens who was sent. He was charged with picking two players whom the Reds would want for their team the following season.

To say he failed is a classic understatement.

Pitching on that Baltimore team at the time were George Herman Ruth and Ernie Shore. Playing shortstop was Claud Derrick. A member of the outfield was George Twombly.

Stevens watched a few games, talked with some Baltimore officials and made his decision. He would take shortstop Derrick and outfielder Twombly back to Cincinnati.

No, he wasn't interested in the fellow named Ruth or the other pitcher named Shore. He would take the shortstop and outfielder.

What a selection!

Derrick's career with the Reds lasted two games. Three days after arriving in Cincinnati, Derrick was shuffled off to the Chicago Cubs for first baseman Fred Mollwitz, who went on to bat .162 for the Reds the remainder of the 1914 season.

Twombly stuck around a little longer, but he, too, had a poor career in Cincinnati. He batted .233 in 1914 and .197 the next year. After appearing in three games in 1916, he was gone from Cincinnati.

The Boston Red Sox also had a working agreement with the Baltimore club. After the Reds had their chance at two players, Boston made its selections. The Boston scout was considerably more efficient. He took a pair of pitchers back to Boston.

Ruth was one of the pitchers and Shore the other. Ruth, as everyone knows, went on to become an outstanding pitcher before he turned home-run-hitting outfielder with the New York Yankees. Shore was not as accomplished as Ruth but in four seasons after going to Boston from Baltimore, he won 56 games — certainly enough to have pleased Reds fans in those days.

Had Babe Ruth originally played major league baseball with the Cincinnati Reds, his career might have been drastically different. He might never have become an outfielder. His pitching prowess might not have been fully developed.

But Reds followers will have to always wonder what might have been.

The biggest bat in baseball, George Herman Ruth, was overlooked in 1914 by a Cincinnati scout who settled for a shortstop and an outfielder on the International League Baltimore club.

When Babe Was Almost A Manager
LARRY MacPHAIL

Babe Ruth, baseball's legendary home-run hitter, had one great desire that remained unfulfilled throughout his long and storied career: He wanted to be a major league manager.

That nearly happened in Cincinnati.

The year was 1934. Owen "Donie" Bush had skippered the Reds in 1933 and had failed miserably. The Reds had finished last, winning only 58 games. The turnstiles were quiet. Cincinnati had drawn only a shade over 218,000 fans. General manager Larry MacPhail wanted to change things around.

Bush was dismissed as manager and MacPhail looked for a new Reds leader. He thought seriously about Babe Ruth. Had MacPhail been able to secure Ruth's release from the New York Yankees, the Bambino would have been installed as the Cincinnati manager for the 1934 season.

MacPhail first became interested in Ruth when an American League club owner told the Reds general manager that Yankees owner Jake Ruppert had agreed to give Ruth his release in order to manage.

At one time there appeared to be three spots open for Ruth: Chicago, Boston and Detroit. But these were filled — Lew Fonseca went to the White Sox, Bucky Harris went to the Red Sox and Mickey Cochrane went to the Tigers.

MacPhail's informant told him that Ruth said he would be willing to manage a club for a salary of $35,000.

"This may look like a large sum," the club owner reportedly told MacPhail, "but you would make it up during your training trip and on your first jaunt around the circuit. Ruth has never played in the National League and he would be a wonderful drawing card so long as he is able to play right field.

"I believe that it would be a good investment for you and that Ruth would be a first-class manager, even if he played only 50 games or so during the season."

MacPhail was convinced. He wanted Ruth and set a plan in motion to secure his services.

He asked his American League friend to find out if Ruppert would release Ruth to the Reds.

The answer came quickly. "No."

MacPhail was told that Ruppert would let the Babe go to any other American League club, but would not send him to the National League. The American League didn't want to lose a big drawing card.

That's as close as Ruth ever came to becoming a major league manager. He eventually traveled to the National League as a player with the Boston Braves. Later he was a coach with the Braves and Dodgers. But the chance to manage a major league team eluded him.

When MacPhail failed to land Ruth as his 1934 manager, he selected Bob O'Farrell, a catcher with the Cardinals. O'Farrell failed to last the season, and he was replaced by Charles Dressen who managed the Reds until Bill McKechnie came in 1938.

Babe Ruth looks more like the club manager he wanted to be than the giant, all-time hitter that he was. He almost managed the Reds in 1934, but the Yankees wouldn't let him go.

When The Reds Ink Turned Black
POWEL CROSLEY

Automobiles were his first love. As a young man, he took a job as a chauffeur so he could work with cars. He nearly raced in the first Indianapolis 500. Later, he manufactured the first small-size American car, which bore his name.

He built refrigerators, making the famous "Shelvador."

Radio caught his fancy and he constructed a transmitter at his home. It evolved into one of the most powerful radio stations in the United States.

But never in his wildest imagination did Powel Crosley ever consider owning a major league baseball franchise. That is, until he was convinced to buy the Reds to insure that the team remain in Cincinnati.

Before buying the club in 1934 at the urging of Larry MacPhail, the team's general manager, Crosley had been interested primarily in automobiles. He built his first car at age 13. After graduation from the University of Cincinnati, where he studied law and engineering, Crosley built a car to race at Indianapolis. Just before the race, he suffered a broken arm and he had to abandon his race plans.

When the automobile business waned, Crosley established a mail-order auto specialty company. Quickly the sales boomed, reaching more than $1 million annually.

Crosley turned to phonographs and his company became a successful producer of the early-model record players. Then, in the early 1920s, radio became his passion.

When his nine-year-old son, Powel Crosley III, wanted a radio receiver and the elder Powel found that one cost $135, he said: "That's a lot of money for a radio, son. Suppose we buy the parts and make our own."

He did. The resulting $35 radio became the forerunner of the Crosley radio which would later become a symbol throughout the world. In no time this manufacturing genius was the world's largest producer of radio receivers, making more than 500 sets a day.

Always thinking ahead, Crosley reasoned that if there were more radio stations on the air, he could sell more sets, so he founded his own station in 1921, constructing it for $250 at his home in the Cincinnati suburb of College Hill, a village just north of the city.

That radio station, known as "The Nation's Station," became one of the country's landmarks. Today, WLW in Cincinnati is a booming, 50,000-watt voice that can be heard via its clear-channel signal over much of the country. It remains the flagship station of the Reds radio network.

With his radio interests and a vibrant automobile accessory company, Crosley was Depression-proof. His was one of the most diversified companies in Cincinnati in the early 1930s. But it would become even more expanded after Crosley met MacPhail late in 1933.

The Depression had crippled the Cincinnati Reds and the club had fallen into receivership to a local bank. The ballclub desperately needed a patron saint. It was widely speculated that the franchise might even be moved to another city if a new Cincinnati owner couldn't be found.

After several meetings, MacPhail convinced Crosley that the purchase of the Reds would be a wise venture, one that would be met with great approval in the community.

Talking later in a newspaper interview, Crosley said, "I simply did not want to see Cincinnati become a minor-league town.

Reds owner Powel Crosley (far right) sits beside manager Birdie Tebbetts and general manager Gabe Paul before a game in 1956.

Cincinnati is the birthplace of professional baseball and it deserves to have a major-league team."

The Reds became much more than a civic gesture in the eyes of Crosley. He put the franchise back on its feet. Five years after Crosley bought the team, the Reds won the pennant. The next year they were the World Champions.

Several times during Crosley's ownership there were reports that the Reds would leave Cincinnati. In the mid-1950s, before there was any major league baseball on the West Coast, Crosley was offered more than $2 million for the franchise by a Los Angeles group. In 1960 it was reported that a $7 million television contract was offered to lure the Reds to New York City. But Crosley steadfastly refused to sell, preferring to keep the Reds in Cincinnati.

Powel Crosley owned and operated the Cincinnati Reds for 27 years. He was still the club president when he died at the age of 74 in 1961.

Even though the ballpark that bore his name, Crosley Field, no longer stands in Cincinnati's West End, he'll be remembered forever for keeping professional baseball's oldest team in Cincinnati.

The Night The Lights Came On
MAY 24, 1935, GAME

"There is no chance of night baseball ever becoming popular in the bigger cities. People there are educated to see the best there is and will stand for only the best. High-class baseball cannot be played at night under artificial light. Furthermore, the benefits derived from attending the game are largely due to fresh air and sunshine. Night air and electric light are a poor substitute."

Those were the words of Clark Griffith, the one-time Cincinnati Reds pitcher and manager who later owned the Washington Senators. He was commenting about night baseball being introduced into the major leagues in 1935 by the Cincinnati Reds.

The first documentation of a night game is June 2, 1883, in Fort Wayne, Indiana, but not one official professional league game was played under the arcs until 1930 when lights were installed at the Independence, Kansas, ballpark. Within weeks other clubs began installing lights, including the Columbus, Ohio, franchise which was owned by Larry MacPhail.

MacPhail, one of the greatest innovators baseball has ever seen, recognized from the beginning that night ball would improve attendance. And when he became general manager of the Reds in 1933, he began an immediate drive to put lights into the Cincinnati ballpark. When Powel Crosley Jr. purchased the club, MacPhail put the bug in his ear.

At first, other baseball owners refused to listen. They insisted that MacPhail had a screw loose. But when Cincinnati's attendance kept declining, baseball's other owners relented and granted permission for the Reds to install lights at Redland Field.

Before the 1935 season, lights went up: 632 lamps turned the Redland Field darkness into near-daylight, and the machinery was in motion for the first major league game under lights.

It was scheduled for May 23 when the Reds were to meet the Philadelphia Phillies. It was a historic occasion. Special electrical arrangements were made for President Franklin D. Roosevelt to throw the switch that would turn darkness into light.

When it came time for the first scheduled night game, Mother Nature upstaged MacPhail and the Reds. Day-long rains caused postponement for 24 hours. Finally, on May 24, 1935, major league baseball's first night game was played.

A crowd of 20,422 was on hand. The attendance was some 10 times more than could have been expected had the two clubs played a day game.

Paul Derringer was the winning pitcher, out-dueling the Phillies Joe Bowman, 2-1. Baseball ushered in a new era.

It wasn't long before Clark Griffith was eating his words. In less than 13 years all major league parks with the exception of Chicago's Wrigley Field had lights.

Night baseball had arrived. Today, it's as much as part of the game as a strikeout or a home run.

The Reds hosted the major league's first night baseball game, in 1935, at Crosley Field.

A First-Base Prize That Got Away
JOHNNY MIZE

When Johnny Mize, the hulking slugger who was known as "The Big Cat," was named to the Hall of Fame in March 1981, it revived memories of how close he came to being a Cincinnati Reds first baseman instead of a St. Louis Cardinal.

After the 1935 season, the Reds were looking for a first baseman to replace the aging Jim Bottomley. Bottomley was a Hall-of-Famer himself, but way past the best days of his career. His successor appeared to be George McQuinn, whom the Reds had plucked out of the New York Yankees farm system.

General manager Larry MacPhail wasn't satisfied and he hoped to find a better player.

During spring training of 1936, MacPhail brought a 23-year-old Georgia native into camp. Johnny Mize, a slugger of tremendous minor league reputation, was sent to the Reds by the St. Louis Cardinals on a look-and-see proposition.

If MacPhail liked what he saw, Mize would play for the Reds. If not, MacPhail could return Mize to the Cardinals.

The Reds took a long, hard look. They liked what they saw. But there were two problems:

The Cardinals wanted $55,000 for Mize's contract, a huge sum during the Depression.

Mize had a knee problem, and MacPhail was worried about what might happen in the future.

At the end of spring training, the Reds shipped Mize back to the Cardinals and put McQuinn at first base.

It would prove to be a big mistake.

Although McQuinn was a good fielder, he couldn't hit and he played only 38 games in 1936, batting .201. He was sent to the minors for more work. He returned to the major leagues in 1938 as a .300 hitter with the St. Louis Browns.

To replace McQuinn in 1937, the Reds went to Les Scarsella, a product of the Cincinnati farm system. He was a better hitter than McQuinn, batting .313 his first year with the Reds.

The Cincinnati first base position, however, remained unsettled until Frank McCormick took over in 1938. That spot in the Reds lineup would remain in good hands until 1946 when McCormick was traded to Philadelphia.

Meanwhile, Mize returned to the Cardinals and broke into the majors with a bang. His knee came around without surgery. In his rookie year Mize batted .329. He hit .364 the next year. For nine consecutive seasons, he batted at least .302. Like many of the game's best players, he missed three years because of World War II.

When he ended his career in 1953, Mize owned a .312 lifetime average, had hit 359 home runs and enjoyed one of the highest slugging averages of anyone who ever played.

He might have compiled those records in a Reds uniform had Larry MacPhail and the Reds taken a chance.

A young Johnny Mize works out with the Reds during spring training in 1936 at Plant Field in Tampa, Florida. Mize was returned to the Cardinals and went on to have a Hall-of-Fame career.

The Builder Of The "Roughhouse"
CHARLES DRESSEN

For a few years in the 1930s, the Cincinnati Reds were known as the "Roughhouse Reds" around the National League. It was their aggressive, hustling, scrappy style of play under new manager Charles Dressen that caused sportswriters to give them the nickname.

Dressen, a one-time quarterback on George Halas' Decatur Staleys — now the Chicago Bears — knew only one brand of baseball: fire and brimstone. He molded his club in that manner. It was Dressen's motto that if the Reds couldn't win the baseball game, at least they could win the fight.

A third baseman with average ability, Dressen played for Cincinnati from 1925 through 1931. Out of a job, he was contemplating joining the police force in his native Decatur, Illinois, when he learned that the Nashville minor league team was about to change managers in early 1932. Always wanting to manage, Dressen went to the Tennessee capital and applied for the job.

His approach to the situation was somewhat unique. He offered to manage without pay if his team didn't win more games than it lost. The Nashville owner was impressed and hired Dressen as a rookie manager. True to his word, Dressen's team won more than it lost, but barely. The club had to win its final game to guarantee Dressen a salary.

Dressen's reputation began to grow. Reds general manager Larry MacPhail wanted to boot Bob O'Farrell as the Reds manager during the 1934 season so he began looking for a replacement. He went to Nashville and recruited Dressen, whose team had won the first half of the Southern League season by seven games. Dressen was hired and reported to the Reds on July 29, 1934.

A laissez-faire attitude had evolved under O'Farrell, but that changed immediately when Dressen joined the club. He shook up the lineup and played a new game. His team bunted a lot, played the hit-and-run game and he used the squeeze play to get the man home from third.

Dressen never had much to work with in Cincinnati during those Depression years, but he did get the Reds out of the cellar and up to fifth in 1936. The following year, though, things got out of hand and he was fired after the 1937 season, when the Reds finished last.

The 1937 campaign was a strange one. The Reds fought more and won less. So enamored of the idea of having a bunch of bullies on his club, Dressen had one player, catcher Gus Brittain, on the team for one specific purpose — to act as a policeman. But the only guy that Brittain fought with that year was his own teammate, pitcher Paul Derringer.

That fight happened before a game when Derringer was warming up and Brittain was catching him. Several of Derringer's curve balls broke sharply into the dirt, hitting Brittain on the unprotected shins.

"If you'd use that much stuff in a game, maybe you could get somebody out," Brittain suggested. Derringer took the barb as a joke and continued to warm up. But quickly he realized Brittain wasn't kidding as the verbal onslaught continued.

Derringer rushed off the mound, grabbed Brittain's mask and hit the catcher over the head with it. That

Manager Charles Dressen poses with general manager Larry MacPhail (left) and Reds owner Powel Crosley Jr. in 1935. Dressen managed the Reds from 1935 through 1937.

ended the fight, and if it hadn't been for that one incident, Gus Brittain would never have been heard of.

After managing the Reds, Dressen was a coach and then returned as a manager with the Brooklyn Dodgers. It was his club that the New York Giants caught in 1951 when they won the pennant on Bobby Thomson's "home run heard 'round the world."

Dressen later managed the Washington Senators, Milwaukee Braves and Detroit Tigers. He died in August of 1966, not long after leaving the post as the Tigers manager.

How A Commissioner Was Picked
WARREN GILES

From Tiskilwa, Illinois, to Cincinnati, Ohio — that is the path Warren Giles took in becoming one of the great baseball executives.

Returning to his small hometown near Moline on the Iowa border after a stint with the United States Army in World War I, Giles began a lifelong association with baseball in 1920 when he became general manager of the Moline club of the Three I League.

From Moline he went to St. Joseph, Missouri, then on to Syracuse, and, finally to his last minor league stop in Rochester in 1927. He built the Rochester team into one of the minor league's mightiest. He generated so much respect that league directors elected him president of the International League while he was still general manager of the Rochester club of that league. They knew he could separate league business from personal business.

Giles came to Cincinnati late in 1936. He was tapped by Reds owner Powel Crosley to succeed Larry MacPhail as general manager. Crosley had known Giles for two years, the two having met at a dinner in Cleveland at the 1935 All-Star game. Giles had made such an impression on Crosley that Crosley knew at the time who would someday be a Cincinnati general manager.

It didn't take long for Giles to exert a positive influence. Cincinnati finished last in 1937, Giles' first year, but in that year he began to clean house and to plan for the future.

Bill McKechnie was brought in as manager. The Reds minor league system was beefed up and Giles began leaning harder and harder on it. He made a few trades. By the end of the 1938 campaign, the Reds had moved up to fourth, their highest finish in 12 years.

The Reds won the pennant in 1939, their first in 20 years. They repeated in 1940 and went on to win the World Championship, beating the Detroit Tigers in seven games.

Cincinnati didn't win another pennant during Giles' tenure as general manager, but the Reds always had a representative club on the field and they consistently finished closer to the top than to the bottom of the division.

Giles nearly became baseball commissioner in 1951, but at the last minute he bowed out of the running and Ford Frick got the position.

How Giles bowed out is a fascinating story in the history of baseball and of the Reds:

In December 1950, baseball's club owners refused to renew the contract of commissioner A. B. "Happy" Chandler. They began to search for a successor. Giles was one popular choice. Ford Frick, a former sportswriter who was president of the National League, was another favorite.

In September 1951, club owners met in Chicago to pick their new commissioner. Giles and Frick were the only two candidates voted on.

It took 12 votes to be elected. Neither could muster that strength.

"The election really was a very seesaw affair," New York Yankees owner Del Webb told the Associated Press after the meeting. "At first Giles was strong, and then suddenly, as new ballots were taken, Frick became stronger."

But Frick still did not have the needed votes. It appeared that the election was hopelessly deadlocked.

"It was a tough decision to make," Giles later recalled. "But after learning from John Galbreath (owner of the Pittsburgh Pirates)

Cincinnati general manager Warren Giles signs manager Luke Sewell to a contract in 1950. The following year Giles became president of the National League.

that the meeting was hopelessly deadlocked, I decided to try and do something about it.

"I asked Galbreath for a few minutes to think over the matter. I then retired to the bathroom in my suite and, after dousing my face several times with handfuls of cold water, I arrived at my decision to retire in favor of Frick. It was just as simple as that."

"Giles made a great stand at the end," Webb said. "Then he came into the meeting room, saw there was a deadlock and declared that he would withdraw and Frick should be the man.

"At that point another ballot was taken and the vote was 14-2 in favor of Frick. A motion was then made to make it unanimous, and on the last ballot Frick received the 16 votes."

With Frick gone as National League President, Giles was his logical successor. He quit as the Reds president in late 1951 and he was unanimously elected league head. He governed league affairs from his office in Cincinnati's Carew Tower until he retired in 1969. He was given the title of President Emeritus. He died in February 1979, regarded as one of the all-time great baseball executives.

The Manager Who Read The Book
DEACON BILL McKECHNIE

Soft-spoken and fatherly, Deacon Bill McKechnie, who led the Cincinnati Reds to two straight pennants in 1939 and 1940, was one of the most respected managers in baseball history.

As a manager, McKechnie's secret to success was in perfecting fine defensive teams and teaching players — in McKechnie's words — to play "better than they knew how."

He was called a book manager, which means he followed the classic elements of the game in all his maneuvers, playing the game by the percentage.

"A book manager?" McKechnie said in an interview in *The Saturday Evening Post* in 1940. "Well, what does that mean? If it means taking advantage of obvious opportunities, pulling your infield in for a play at the plate, moving it back for a double play, waiting out wild or tiring pitchers, bunting on poor-fielding pitchers, running on catchers who can't throw, sending men home on weak-armed outfielders; if that's what it means, I plead guilty. I am a book manager. Show me a manager who isn't and I'll show you a manager who loses a lot of games he ought to win."

McKechnie won more than his share in a managerial career that began in 1922 and continued through 1946. He's the only manager to take three different teams to the World Series, winning with the Cardinals, the Pirates and twice with the Reds.

It was with the Reds that he enjoyed his greatest success which led to his induction in 1962 into baseball's Hall of Fame.

Team general manager Warren Giles and Reds owner Powel Crosley Jr. teamed up to bring McKechnie to Cincinnati in 1938. The Reds had finished last the previous year under Charles Dressen and a change was in order.

McKechnie was at the end of his contract with the Boston Braves, whom he had managed for eight seasons. He had gained quite a reputation, keeping a near-bankrupt and talent-short team in contention most of the time. As many as four teams were trying to lure McKechnie away from the Braves.

Meanwhile in Cincinnati, the fans were restless and picked their own man. The populace wanted Hazen "Ki-Ki" Cuyler, a veteran outfielder who finished his playing career with the Reds. The city was overwhelmed with "We-Want-Cuyler" petitions. Before paying the fare on a streetcar, the passenger was asked to sign a petition in support of Cuyler.

But Giles and Crosley wanted McKechnie. And they got him.

"You must wait and see," Giles said. "This fellow's the best manager in baseball. He'll bring us a championship in two years at least. Maybe even this year."

Indeed, McKechnie was good. The 1938 Reds went from last place to fourth, and came close to winning the pennant. They finished only six games behind the champion Cubs. They might have won had not left-handed pitcher Lee Grissom broken his ankle late in the season while trying to steal a base.

The following two years the Reds did win the pennant. In 1939 Cincinnati wasn't the top run-producer under McKechnie. But the Reds allowed the fewest, a testament to his brand of baseball. They beat the St. Louis Cardinals by 4½ games. The next year it was a runaway as McKechnie's club finished 12 games ahead of Brooklyn.

McKechnie stayed with the Reds through the 1946 season. He never won another pennant, but he consistently had the Reds near the top. Until Sparky Anderson

Continued on page 86

Manager Bill McKechnie looks to the heavens before a game at Crosley Field in 1939. McKechnie piloted the Reds that season to their first pennant in 20 years.

Reds manager Bill McKechnie meets a Cincinnati manager of another era, Charles "Chick" Fulmer, who was the Reds manager in 1882. They got together before an old-timers game in Philadelphia in 1939.

Continued from page 84

managed the team in the 1970s, McKechnie's reign was the longest in the club history. His Reds victory total of 747 was No. 1 until Anderson also broke that mark.

Bill McKechnie was one of those kinds of people who earned respect from everyone. Almost everybody called him Mr. McKechnie, regardless of how well they knew the man. He also was known as Deacon Bill because of his strong ties to the Methodist Church.

He had his ups and downs in a professional baseball career that began in the early 1900s. He played parts of 11 years in the major leagues as a utility infielder, including portions of two years with the Reds, coming to Cincinnati along with Christy

The six umpires and two managers meet before the first game of the 1940 World Series at Crosley Field. The Reds manager is Bill McKechnie. Detroit's manager is Del Baker.

Mathewson in a trade with the New York Giants.

He once was fired after winning the pennant. That came in 1928 when his Cardinals were beaten in four straight games by the New York Yankees in the World Series. The St. Louis owner knew he had made a mistake, however, and before the 1929 season was finished, he had McKechnie back in St. Louis.

Deacon Bill wouldn't leave the major league scene again until he retired after the 1949 season, spending his last three years in uniform as a coach for the Cleveland Indians.

He retired to Bradenton, Florida, and lived there until he died of leukemia in 1965.

A No-Hitter Follows A No-Hitter
JOHNNY VANDER MEER

"It's only fair to warn Adolf Hitler that if he does march in Czechoslovakia one of these fine hot days, he won't have the headlines in these parts if the Reds are playing — and particularly if Johnny Vander Meer is in the box."
Cincinnati Enquirer editorial,
June 17, 1938

That editorial appeared two days after the left-handed-throwing Vander Meer performed the most incredible pitching feat baseball has ever seen — back-to-back no-hitters. On June 15, working the first night game ever played at Ebbetts Field in Brooklyn, Vandy held the Dodgers hitless, matching his previous start four days earlier when he fired a no-hitter against Boston.

The first one, an afternoon game against the Boston Bees at Crosley Field in Cincinnati, was a 3-0 masterpiece. He faced only 28 batters and not one Boston player reached second base in the first Cincinnati no-hitter since 1919.

The second one was tougher. Vander Meer, who was plagued by wildness throughout his career, walked five through the first eight innings but appeared to be throwing the ball much harder than in the first no-hitter. The Reds built a six-run lead and then awaited the fateful ninth.

After getting out Buddy Hassett, who led off the ninth, Vander Meer suddenly couldn't throw a strike. He walked the next three batters — Babe Phelps, Cookie Lavagetto and Dolf Camilli. That brought manager Bill McKechnie out of the dugout for some comforting words.

McKechnie's advice obviously helped. Ernie Koy was the next hitter and he bounced a ground ball to third baseman Lew Riggs. Riggs threw home to catcher Ernie Lombardi for a force out. All that stood between Vander Meer and immortality was Leo Durocher.

Durocher, for whom the expression "good field, no hit" was probably invented, didn't spoil Vander Meer's night of nights. Leo hit a short fly to center that was easily grabbed by Harry Craft.

Ironically, Vander Meer had at one time been a member of both the Boston and the Brooklyn organizations. Because of a paper-work mistake, Brooklyn lost him and Boston sold his contract to Nashville in the Southern League in 1936.

Nashville offered the Dutch Master to the Boston Red Sox for $25,000, but was turned down. Bill Terry, manager of the New York Giants, wanted the left-hander, but was willing to pay only $15,000. That was snubbed by Nashville.

Finally, the Reds offered $15,000 plus a player and Vander Meer joined the Reds farm team in Durham, North Carolina. He was voted the top minor league player in 1936 and that earned him a promotion to the major leagues in 1937. But the 22-year-old southpaw had repeated control problems and finally was optioned to Syracuse to try to get his pitching act together. Wildness kept him in the hole.

New manager McKechnie began working immediately in the spring of 1938 on Vander Meer's control problems. Nothing seemed to work, so McKechnie and coach Hank Gowdy arranged a meeting with Lefty Grove, the former great Philadelphia hurler who, like Vander Meer, had severe control problems as a young pitcher.

Grove's advice to Vander Meer was simple: follow through more.

"I was wild," Grove explained to Vandy, "because I was letting the ball go too soon and not following through. So I decided to follow through with my pitch regardless of where the ball went. I made myself follow through to the extent that I didn't consider any pitch properly executed unless my left forearm struck my right knee after letting the ball go.

"I actually bruised my left forearm by constantly practicing this method of delivery. But I achieved what I was after...."

Vander Meer's control began coming around and McKechnie worked his young pitcher slowly into the rotation. By early June he was as solid as a rock. Then came the two no-hitters.

But this is not a fairy tale and all did not live happily ever after. Vandy was 15-10 in the double no-hit season of 1938, but the next year he was only 5-9. The year after that he found himself in the minor leagues.

Vander Meer did make it back, winning 49 games in the next three seasons and also leading the National League in strikeouts those three years. But he never quite became the kind of pitcher it looked like he would be when he threw the two no-hitters at the age of 24.

Vander Meer pitched with the Reds through the 1949 season, pitched with the Chicago Cubs in 1950 and wound up his major league career in 1951 working one game with the Cleveland Indians.

He lost more games, 121, than he won, 119, but in two consecutive starts in 1938, no one has ever been better.

This framed picture was made when Johnny Vander Meer hurled back-to-back no-hitters in 1938. The box scores are in the lower portion of the photo.

To The Mound By Way Of Third
BUCKY WALTERS

Johnny Vander Meer's first no-hitter grabbed all the newspaper headlines on June 12, 1938, but a small story elsewhere in the sports section that day reported of a trade that would have a significant impact on the Cincinnati Reds in future years.

Earlier that day — prior to Vander Meer's no-hitter at Ebbetts Field in Brooklyn — Reds general manager Warren Giles had engineered a trade with the Philadelphia Phillies.

Had Vander Meer not made history with his second no-hit game, the story of the trade which brought Bucky Walters to the Reds might have gotten the big bold headlines.

Walters was a third-baseman-turned-pitcher, but he had accomplished little for the Phillies. He led the National League in losses in 1936 with 21 and had only a 4-8 won-and-lost record when the Reds acquired him. But Bill McKechnie, the foxy Cincinnati field manager, felt Walters was about to bloom into one of baseball's best pitchers.

And that's exactly what the big right-hander did.

Three times he became a 20-game winner for the Reds. He helped pitch them to a pair of National League pennants. In 1939 he was voted the National League's Most Valuable Player when he won 27 games and posted a league-leading earned run average of 2.27.

Had it not been for Jimmie Wilson, Walters' former manager in Philadelphia, however, Bucky never would have become a major league pitcher and would be remembered only by the most devout Phillies fans as a decent-fielding, light-hitting third baseman.

Wilson, impressed with Walters' strong throws from third to first, forced Walters to make the move to the mound during spring training in 1935.

Walters resisted the move. "But I don't know anything about pitching," he told Wilson, who later related the incident to New York sportswriter Harold Parrott.

"You've got a month of this spring training season left to learn," Wilson said. "As a third baseman, you'll starve."

Bucky had been acquired by the Phillies from the Boston Red Sox and he was hitting only .216 when he went to Philadelphia during the 1934 season. He batted .250 for Philadelphia the rest of the year, but when Johnny Vergez was brought in to play third base in a trade with the Giants, Walters' days as an infielder were doomed.

As an incentive, Wilson offered Walters a $25 bonus for every game he won. That was enough to convince Bucky to take the mound.

Walters had a strong and supple arm. He threw a natural sinker. He possessed the perfect combination to make an outstanding pitcher. For a while, it looked like he never would be able to realize his potential. But when he got to Cincinnati, his fortunes changed. Jimmie Wilson played a role there, too.

The Phillies fired Wilson after the 1938 season and he was hired by the Reds as a coach in 1939. His influence on Walters was never greater. Bucky even wound up pitching to Wilson when the latter was forced to become activated in 1940 because of an injury to regular catcher Ernie Lombardi.

Walters, a native Philadelphian, broke into professional baseball in 1929 with High Point, North Carolina, in the Piedmont League. During that rookie season, he played every position except catcher. At the end of the season his contract was purchased by the Boston Braves.

Bucky Walters (right) and Paul Derringer embrace after pitching the Reds to the National League pennant in 1939. They combined to win 52 games that season.

He played briefly as an infielder with the Braves at the end of the 1931 season. After a strong year in 1933 in the Pacific Coast League, he went to the Red Sox. Then it was on to his rendezvous with Wilson in Philadelphia for the eventual change that would leave Walters extremely grateful.

Bucky pitched nine full seasons with the Reds. In 1948 he became the club's manager and held that position for two years. After that he went to the Braves as a pitching coach and retired from baseball in the mid-1950s.

Bucky Walters is remembered in Cincinnati as one of the best pitchers ever for the Reds, but had it not been for Jimmie Wilson's uncanny perception, Bucky Walters probably would have ended up as an unknown back home in Philadelphia.

The Kickin' That Overcame Lickin'
PAUL DERRINGER

The first year that this big, tall right-hander ever put on a Cincinnati Reds uniform, he lost 27 games — the largest total in major league baseball in 28 years.

But before his Cincinnati career ended, Paul Derringer was cheered and idolized. He is remembered as one of the all-time greats who pitched in Cincinnati.

Early in the 1933 season, Derringer was traded by the St. Louis Cardinals to the Reds for shortstop Leo Durocher. The Cardinals needed help on the infield because of an injury to Charley Gelbert. The Reds were eager to get a young, hard-throwing pitcher in exchange for a shortstop who had a reputation of being "good field, no hit."

Derringer, a rookie sensation in 1931 when he led the league in winning percentage with a .692 on the strength of an 18-8 record, dropped to 11-14 in 1932. He was 0-2 with the Red Birds when the trade was made.

Big Paul was a right-hander with a big kick. He was anything but successful when he came to the Reds. Cincinnati was a last-place team and Derringer fell into a losing pattern, finishing with a 7-27 record. He learned a lot, however, and the experience of that dismal season would pay off in the future.

"I look back on that season of 1933 as one of my best in the majors. They licked me time after time, but I pitched well. I think in about 19 games I was beaten when I allowed an average of about three runs per game. The Cincinnati club that year was terrible. I hate to say it, but I think it was about the worst I ever played on," Derringer said when asked to remember his maiden season with the Reds.

Two years after losing 27 games, Derringer came back to win 22, the first of four 20-victory seasons he would have in Cincinnati.

When the Reds won the pennant in 1939 and 1940, Derringer played a big role. He was a 25-game winner in 1939 and followed with 20 victories in 1940.

He teamed with Bucky Walters, another right-hander, to form the best one-two punch in baseball. Between them in those two pennant-winning seasons, they won 94 games and lost only 40.

Derringer was a control artist and he rarely walked a batter. Take the 1939 campaign, for instance. He pitched 301 innings and walked only 35 batters. As incredible as it seems, 24 of those 35 free passes were intentional walks.

Paul's control was sensational. Once, as a stunt before a ball game, he took the mound blindfolded and delivered six of 10 pitches over the plate for strikes.

Derringer credited Hall-of-Fame pitcher Grover Cleveland Alexander for his pinpoint accuracy.

"When I reported to the Cardinals, Alex (Alexander) was there. Despite the fact that he had been a World Series hero the year before, Alex was one of the few who took pains to help me. He drilled one thought home, 'If you have something on the ball, control is the main thing.' I've never forgotten that pitching proverb and it had a lot to do with shaping my career."

Derringer was long considered one of the best "money" pitchers in the game, meaning he could always be counted on to come through in the clutch situation. Because of that reputation, it was hard to figure out how he lost his first four decisions in World Series play — two with the Cardinals in 1931, one in the 1939 World Series and the opening game of the 1940 Fall Classic.

However, with everything on the line in Game No. 7 of the 1940 Series, he was indeed superb. He beat Bobo Newsom, 2-1, to nail down Cincinnati's first World Championship in 21 years.

Derringer pitched in Cincinnati through the 1942 season and then was traded to the Chicago Cubs. He finished his 15-year career in Chicago in 1945, having won 223 games.

He retired to Sarasota, Florida, where he makes his home today.

The high kick of the right leg was a familiar trademark of Cincinnati right-hander Paul Derringer, winner of 20 or more games four times with the Reds.

A First-Class Player On Third
BILL WERBER

After moving from eighth to fourth place in 1938, the Cincinnati Reds were favored to keep going and win the National League pennant in 1939. But there was a chink in the armor. The team needed a third baseman.

Lew Riggs had been the regular since 1935, but he was only an average fielder and a .250 hitter. Manager Bill McKechnie desperately needed to replace him.

Meanwhile, the Philadelphia Athletics were having problems with their crackerjack third baseman, Bill Werber. He was rebelling against a $2,000 salary cut and had not reported to spring training. Werber was determined to stay home until he got the salary he wanted.

Philadelphia owner and manager Connie Mack began shopping Werber around to American League clubs but found no one wanting a third baseman who had batted only .259 the year before. Finally Mack asked waivers on Werber to see if any National League teams had an interest. When the Reds were informed, McKechnie and general manager Warren Giles immediately went after Werber. They believed he would be the answer to their problems and they were right.

Bill Werber, a product of Duke University, had gained a reputation in the American League as a somewhat haughty individual, a trouble-maker, a big-headed pop-off who had trouble getting along with his teammates.

But Werber made a different kind of impression when he was sold to the Reds and reported to the team in Tampa for the end of spring training.

"We expected to see a cross between a dyspeptic wildcat and corner-lot bully," sportswriter Whitney Martin wrote after the Reds won back-to-back pennants in 1939 and 1940. "It was a little discomforting to see a dapper, alert young fellow come bouncing up and respond to a greeting with a friendly grin and an I-mean-it handshake. The little guy just oozed personality, and you know that no matter what he might be like on a ballfield he'd be right at home in a top-hat-and-tails gathering."

Werber spent three years in Cincinnati, batting .289 and .277 in the pennant-winning seasons. He led the National League in runs scored in 1939 with 115, one of the highest single-season performances in Cincinnati history. He was a magnificent fielder and played with intense enthusiasm.

"He was the key man of the Cincinnati infield this year (1940)," Martin wrote, adding, "... the spark which always was there when a blaze was needed. His work in the World Series was sensational, and he at least deserves a place on the honor roll of most valuable players."

The Reds traded Werber to the New York Giants after the 1941 season and he played there for one year before retiring. He returned to his home in suburban Washington, D.C., and began a successful career as an insurance executive.

In 1972 Werber retired again and went to Naples, Florida, where he began writing a book entitled *Circling The Bases.*

"So many books recently have downgraded baseball. I simply thought I would write about the decent people in baseball," Werber said.

Even though he might have been a bit arrogant at one time, Werber was one of those decent people and will be remembered in Cincinnati not only as a standout third baseman but as a first-class person as well.

Third baseman Billy Werber crosses the plate during a Reds game at Crosley Field in 1940. Werber scored 105 runs that season and led the league the year before with 115.

The Backstop Who's Overlooked
ERNIE LOMBARDI

There are a number of former catchers in baseball's Hall of Fame — Gabby Hartnett, Mickey Cochrane, Yogi Berra, Bill Dickey, Ray Schalk and Roger Bresnahan, to name a few.

One more belongs with that select group, but he has never been included. He's Ernie Lombardi, the former Cincinnati catcher who won two batting championships and had a 17-year batting average of .306.

Lombardi currently is not eligible to be installed in baseball's shrine because he generally was ignored by Baseball Writers Association voters during the 20 years of balloting after he retired. But he rates as well as, if not better than, several of the Hall of Fame backstops.

Schalk, for instance, had only a .253 career batting average. Bresnahan, the first catcher to wear shin guards, in 1907, was only a .280 lifetime hitter.

Lombardi's contemporaries were Cochrane, Dickey and Hartnett. Lombardi's career statistics stack up favorably against these catchers. Yet he's been ignored while his three contemporaries have been in the Hall of Fame for years.

Ernie Lombardi was a cartoonist's dream. He was called "The Schnozz" because of his unusually large nose.

"He brought to baseball," wrote baseball historian Lee Allen in *The Cincinnati Reds,* "a nose so lavish in its geography that the more famous schnozzola of Jimmy Durante's seems picayunish in comparison."

Lombardi, son of Italian immigrants, grew up and first played baseball in Oakland, a hotbed of baseball for years. He was originally signed by the Brooklyn Dodgers in 1931, but the following year he was traded to the Reds as part of a six-player exchange. The Reds shipped Clyde Sukeforth, Tom Cuccinello and Joe Stripp to the Dodgers for Lombardi, Wally Gelbert and Babe Herman. It was one of the best trades the Reds ever made.

Lombardi blossomed into an outstanding hitter. In his 10 seasons in Cincinnati, Lombardi batted over .300 in seven of them. In one four-year stretch he batted .343, .333, .334, and .342. The .342 average in 1938 was good enough to win the National League batting championship. When he won the title, he became only the second catcher in modern history to win a batting title — Bubbles Hargrave of the Reds was the other in 1926.

Lombardi's biggest knock was his speed. He might have been the slowest man ever to play major league baseball. Infielders would play so deep on him that it almost appeared there were seven outfielders. On more than one occasion he was thrown out at first base by an outfielder who pegged a perfect throw to first as Ernie slowly trudged down the base path, looking as if a piano were strapped to his backside.

Lombardi long will be remembered for a play in the ninth inning of Game No. 4 of the 1939 World Series with the New York Yankees. The Reds, down three games to none, were attempting a comeback and led, 4-2, in the ninth inning of the fourth contest. But the Reds muffed a double-play ball and the Yankees finally tied the score to send the game into extra innings.

That set the stage for one of the strangest plays ever in World Series competition. Frank Crosetti walked and Charlie Keller was safe on an error bringing Joe DiMaggio to the plate. He promptly singled to right field. When Ival Goodman let the ball get away from him, both Crosetti and Keller scored. In scoring, Keller crashed into Lombardi and knocked him flat on his back. Even though the ball was at his feet, Lombardi couldn't move and DiMaggio was safe at the plate, circling the bases to score the seventh run.

There weren't too many kind things to say about Lombardi after that play. But what was never reported at that time was that Lombardi had been kicked in the groin in the collision with Keller. He couldn't move, let alone pick up the baseball and tag DiMaggio.

Unfortunately, that's how many people remember Ernie Lombardi, flat on his back, rather than being one of the best-hitting catchers in baseball history.

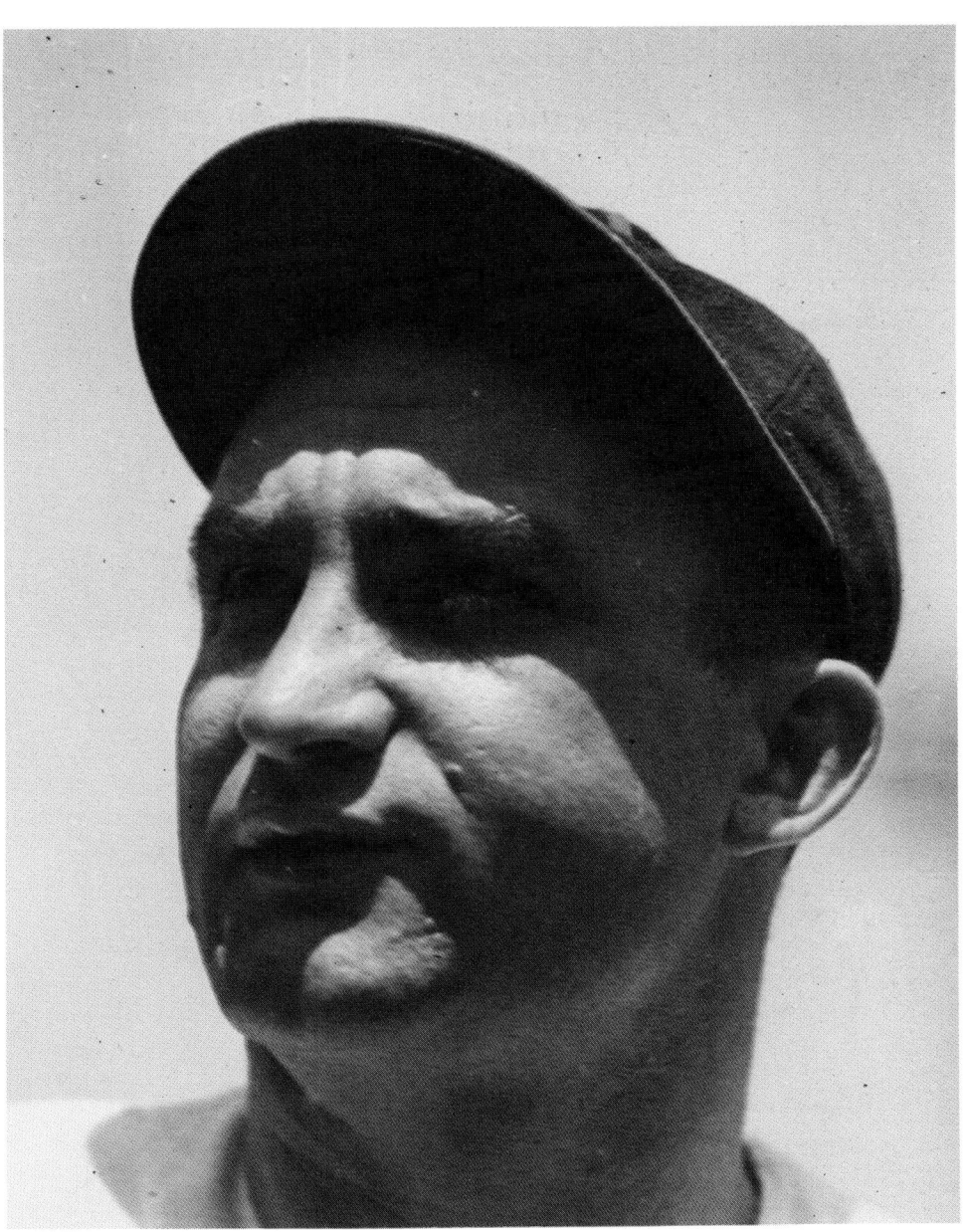

Ernie Lombardi was one of baseball's best catchers, compiling a .306 lifetime batting average and winning two batting championships.

A Catcher's Call And Tragedy
WILLARD HERSHBERGER

The 1940 baseball season in Cincinnati was one of the happiest ever. The Reds won their second straight National League pennant and beat the Detroit Tigers in seven games in the World Series.

But it also will be remembered as a sad year. It was the season when reserve catcher Willard Hershberger took his life while the Reds were on an East Coast road trip.

On the evening of July 31, 1940, the Reds were in first place and playing the New York Giants in the Polo Grounds. Bucky Walters, the Reds big winner, was on the mound and had a 4-1 lead in the ninth inning. Suddenly the Giants got hot. They won the game, 5-4, when Harry Danning blasted a home run.

The game hit Hershberger hard. He was the catcher and took responsibility for calling the wrong pitch to Danning, normally an easy out for Walters.

He was told to forget such feelings, that the game meant nothing and that the Reds still had a comfortable lead. But Hershberger continued to brood.

After two days off, the Reds went into Boston for a double-header with the Braves.

Hershberger caught the second game and was still in a state of despair. The Reds lost both games and Hershberger didn't get a hit in five at bats, unusual because he was batting well over .300 at that time.

Hershberger obviously was troubled. Once, a Boston hitter bunted a pitch about 15 feet out in front of the plate. Hershberger made no effort to field it. Manager Bill McKechnie was stunned and he bolted out of the dugout.

"Is something wrong?" McKechnie asked.

As McKechnie related later, Hershberger answered, "You bet there's something wrong. I'll tell you about it after the game."

After the game McKechnie took Hershberger to dinner. The manager was shocked by what Hershberger told him. The catcher said he was contemplating suicide.

They talked late into the night. It appeared to the manager, when the two men went to their separate rooms, that Hershberger's depression had passed.

The Reds had another double-header scheduled the following day. Hershberger was up early, eating breakfast with *Cincinnati Enquirer* sports editor Lou Smith. Smith later said Hershberger appeared to be in "good spirits."

But when the Reds arrived at the ballpark, Hershberger wasn't in uniform to take batting practice.

Gabe Paul, the club's public relations director and traveling secretary, phoned Hershberger and asked the reason he wasn't in uniform. The answer he got was, "I'm sick."

Hershberger was told to come to the park, that he didn't have to suit up. The catcher agreed.

That was the last time anyone talked with Willard Hershberger.

Hershberger did not show up by the end of the first game, and McKechnie became concerned. He sent Dan Cohen, a Cincinnati fan who often traveled with the Reds, to the hotel to find Hershberger.

When Cohen got to Hershberger's room he found the lifeless body in the bathroom. Hershberger had cut his throat.

There appeared to be no more popular player on the 1940 Reds than Willard Hershberger. He was a tremendous substitute for Ernie Lombardi. He batted .276 in 1938, .345 in 1939 and he was batting .309 in 1940, the last year of his life.

Catcher Willard Hershberger straps on his shin guard before a Reds game in 1940. Later that season he took his life in Boston.

The Coach Who Caught The Series
JIMMIE WILSON

There were many people responsible for the Cincinnati Reds winning the World Series in 1940, but the real hero was a 40-year-old coach who came out of retirement late in the season and played a significant role in the Reds four victories over the Detroit Tigers in the Fall Classic.

Jimmie Wilson was one of baseball's best catchers during the 1920s and 1930s when he caught for the Philadelphia Phillies and the St. Louis Cardinals. He came to the Reds as a coach in 1939, replacing Edd Roush, who had resigned because of contract difficulties.

"Although I've signed as a coach," Wilson told newspaper reporters when he came to Cincinnati, "I feel I can catch some and will be ready whenever I'm needed."

He played in only four games that 1939 season, but late in 1940 his services were badly needed. Ernie Lombardi, the regular catcher and one of baseball's best hitters, suffered a badly sprained ankle on September 15 and was finished for the season. With the suicide of Willard Hershberger, a pair of rookies — Bill Baker and Dick West — stood to do most of the remaining catching.

Wilson had kept himself in shape, so when manager Bill McKechnie asked Wilson to finish out the season behind the plate, Jimmie was ready. He caught the final 16 games of the regular season, getting ready for the World Series. And ready he was. Those creaky, aching muscles held together. Wilson put on a show that ranks as one of the most heroic in Cincinnati history.

Jimmie Wilson caught six of the seven World Series games, was the top Reds hitter, handled Cincinnati's pitching staff with ease and unbelievably stole the only base in the Series.

In the seventh game, when the Reds beat the Tigers, 2-1, to win their first championship since 1919, Wilson had two hits and contributed a key sacrifice in the deciding two-run seventh inning. He was a team player all the way.

Wilson's major league career began in 1923 in Philadelphia. He went to the Cardinals in 1928 and played in two World Series. In 1934 he went back to Philadelphia as a playing manager, and stayed with the Phillies until he resigned after the 1938 season.

"I'm tickled to death with my new job," Wilson said upon arrival in Cincinnati. "But any job would be better than managing the Phils."

In Wilson's four seasons as the Philadelphia manager, the Phillies finished next to last three times and last in 1938. It wasn't Wilson's fault, though. In fact, he earned praises for the Phillies seventh-place finishes and many baseball experts marveled at how he kept the team out of the cellar.

As a manager he was known as an adept handler of pitchers. It was Wilson who made Bucky Walters a pitcher, switching him from a run-of-the-mill third baseman into one of the game's best hurlers in the late 1930s and early 1940s.

And before he signed to coach with the Reds, a number of other major league teams sought Wilson's services. Cleveland, for instance, wanted him as a player-coach so that he could be behind the plate when Bob Feller pitched. Feller, a flame-throwing kid at that time, went on to stardom and was one of the game's best-known strikeout pitchers.

Two years after arriving in Cincinnati, Wilson got another managerial shot, this time with the Chicago Cubs. He was there a little over three years and returned to McKechnie's staff in 1944 to coach again. In 1946 he retired and moved to Bradenton, Florida, where he entered the citrus business. He died the following year of a heart attack.

Some said he passed on because of a broken heart. His only son, Bob, who frequently worked out with the Reds when Wilson was with Cincinnati, was especially close to his father. The younger Wilson was killed in a plane crash in India during World War II. Following that personal tragedy, life didn't hold much joy for Jimmie Wilson.

An outstanding baseball player and a great man died at the age of 47, a few hours after playing a round of golf.

After leaving the Reds, Jimmie Wilson became manager of the Chicago Cubs in 1942. Here he chats with his old friend, Reds skipper Bill McKechnie.

Lucky No. 7, The Fantastic Game 1940 WORLD SERIES

One of the most exciting games ever played in Cincinnati came in 1940 when the Reds won the World Championship at Crosley Field by beating the Detroit Tigers, 2-1, in the seventh game.

Detroit took a 3-2 lead in the Series, winning the fifth game, 8-0, behind the three-single pitching of Bobo Newsom. The Reds evened the count in Game No. 6 when Bucky Walters pitched a shutout and hit a home run in a 4-0 Cincinnati victory.

Those two games set the stage for the climactic seventh. A standing-room-only crowd of 26,854 jammed into cozy Crosley Field.

It was a classic mound matchup. Newsom, pitching with only a day's rest, faced Paul Derringer, the Reds right-hander who had won 20 games during the regular season. The two had been the starters in Game No. 1, a 7-2 decision by Detroit.

Detroit jumped on top with a run in the third inning. Billy Sullivan, the Tiger catcher, singled and went to second on a sacrifice bunt by Newsom. Sullivan scored moments later when third baseman Billy Werber overthrew first base after fielding Charlie Gehringer's hot smash.

Newsom pitched shutout ball for six innings before the Reds could muster anything. In the seventh the Reds got their chance.

First baseman Frank McCormick, the National League's Most Valuable Player with a .309 batting average and a league-leading 44 doubles, drilled his specialty, a double, against the left-field fence to lead off the seventh.

Jimmy Ripple, the left fielder who was acquired midway through the season from Brooklyn and batted .307, followed McCormick to the plate. Ripple sent a long drive to the right-center-field power alley. It looked as though Detroit right fielder Bruce Campbell would catch the ball.

Fearing the catch, McCormick held at second, but, as the ball fell, he headed for home. The Tigers would have had a play at the plate, but shortstop Dick Bartell held Campbell's throw. McCormick scored standing up to tie the game. And Ripple slid into second.

Ripple went to third when catcher Jimmie Wilson sacrificed. That brought a limping Ernie Lombardi out of the dugout to pinch-hit for Eddie Joost, the second baseman. Lombardi was intentionally walked and shortstop Billy Meyers came to bat.

Meyers had walked out on the team earlier in the season because of "personal problems." In Game No. 7 he had no problems. He worked the count to three balls and one strike and then delivered the winning run across the plate.

Meyers hit a long fly ball to center field. Ripple tagged at third base. After Barney McCosky caught the ball for the Tigers, Ripple raced home with the go-ahead run.

Derringer took over, retiring the final six Detroit batters, and Cincinnati won the World Championship.

The Reds were quite adept at winning games in this fashion. During the regular season Cincinnati had won 41 games by a one-run margin and lost only 17. It was a case of almost everyone in the lineup contributing something, a hallmark of the team all season long.

The city of Cincinnati celebrated its World Championship in grand fashion. Automobiles were not allowed to enter the downtown area and crowds spilled into the streets. It was a wild night of celebrating. A streetcar was dismantled. For the most part, however, Cincinnati celebrated with class, savoring its first championship in 21 years. It would be 35 long years before the city would know such a feeling again.

The Cincinnati streets filled with people, cars and confetti after the Reds beat the Detroit Tigers on October 8, 1940, and won the World Series. This scene is Fifth and Vine in Cincinnati.

A Javelin That Was Thrown Away
JOE BEGGS

One of the first highly successful relief specialists in Cincinnati Reds history was right-hander Joe Beggs, a lanky 6-footer. At one time, Beggs was one of America's best javelin throwers.

Beggs burst onto the Cincinnati baseball scene in sensational fashion in 1940 when he became manager Bill McKechnie's most trustworthy pitcher out of the bullpen. Beggs pitched in 37 games — 36 in relief — and allowed only 19 runs in 77 innings. His earned run average of 2.00 was the lowest among National League pitchers who worked more than 75 innings.

He quickly earned the nickname "Fireman Joe."

Beggs attended Geneva College in Beaver Falls, Pennsylvania. He was a better track-and-field performer in his collegiate days than he was a baseball player. The javelin was his specialty. After a standout performance at the prestigious Penn Relays, he was encouraged to work seriously on the javelin. He was told that a spot on the United States Olympic team and a trip to the 1932 Olympics could be in the offing.

Instead he turned to baseball and broke in professionally in Washington, Pennsylvania, in the Penn State League.

Beggs first made it to the major leagues with the New York Yankees in 1938, but the next year he was shipped to the Yankees Class AAA Syracuse farm club.

Beggs appeared to have no future with the New York organization so when the Reds offered pitcher Lee Grissom in a trade for Beggs, the Yankees jumped at it.

While Beggs never had *the* one big winning season, he always was stingy when it came to allowing earned runs. His nine-year major league earned run average was 2.96.

Despite the fact that Beggs was a top-notch relief pitcher, he always wanted to be a starter. In 1943 he got his chance. In four starting assignments, he pitched four complete games. Indeed, he did have a nine-inning arm.

He was set to be one of McKechnie's regulars in the rotation the next year, but he went into the Navy and served two years as a gunnery officer.

Returning to the Reds in 1946, Beggs came back with a flourish. In his first start, he pitched eight innings and allowed the Chicago Cubs only a scratch single. He went on to win 12 games and to post a glittering 2.32 earned run average in 190 innings of work.

"He's at his best under pressure," Reds publicist Gabe Paul, later a Reds general manager, wrote in a press release. "What does Beggs have? He has pretty fair stuff, great control and courage. He doesn't flinch."

But after Beggs' comeback in 1946, age began catching up with him. He was 36 years old in 1947 and after he was 0-3 in 11 games that season, he was traded to the New York Giants for Babe Young. He was 3-3 the remainder of that year with New York. After only one appearance in 1948, Beggs was released; the years had doused the flames for Fireman Joe.

Relief ace Joe Beggs works in the bullpen during spring training in Tampa, Florida. Fireman Joe won 12 and lost only three in his first year with the Reds in 1940.

The Star Who Lost To Gary Cooper
WAITE HOYT

If Hollywood producer Sam Goldwyn hadn't changed his mind, Waite Hoyt might have wound up in the movies instead of behind a microphone as an announcer for the Cincinnati Reds.

When a movie was first planned on the life of Lou Gehrig, the great New York Yankee first baseman, Hoyt was one of the early choices to play the part of Gehrig. Hoyt and Gehrig had played together.

But when the script was written, the movie was considered better than "B" caliber. Goldwyn began assembling a cast with one of Hollywood's premier actors in the lead role. Waite Hoyt lost out to Gary Cooper, who helped make "The Pride Of The Yankees" one of the most outstanding sports movies ever filmed.

Hoyt turned to broadcasting and became one of the big names in the baseball play-by-play field. Starting in 1942, Hoyt was a household name in the Midwest, broadcasting Cincinnati Reds games over the "Burger Beer Baseball Network." The network was one of the biggest of its day and Hoyt was highly respected.

H. G. Salsinger, the noted Detroit sports columnist, was impressed with Hoyt's delivery over the air. Salsinger wrote:

"Hoyt differs from the majority of baseball broadcasters. In the first place, he speaks good English which few of the others do. In the second place, he knows baseball which, again, few of the others do. In the third place, he is interesting, which most of the others are not. In the fourth place, he has a trained voice, which probably none of the others has."

During Hoyt's heyday, baseball fans would often look forward to rain days. He would dazzle his listeners with stories from the days when he played alongside Babe Ruth and Gehrig. He made a record, "Waite Hoyt in the Rain," which became a big seller in the 1950s.

Hoyt came from a stage background and was as much at home talking to people on stage as he was pitching to batters in a baseball game. Hoyt's father had been a singer and monologist in New York.

During his playing career with the New York Yankees, Hoyt went into vaudeville and once played the famous Palace Theatre in New York. He worked on the same bill as an up-and-coming young comedian, Jimmy Durante. Hoyt had ambitions at one time to become a concert singer and he took vocal lessons for several years.

Hoyt was considered a boy wonder when he began his baseball career right from a Brooklyn high school at the age of 15. John McGraw, the feisty manager of the New York Giants, first noticed Hoyt pitch in a sandlot game.

"The great McGraw must have been impressed," wrote Damon Runyon, the New York sportswriter who later became famous as a playwright, "because although Waite was only 15 years old, he was signed to a big-league contract, the youngest player ever to be signed."

Hoyt didn't get along with McGraw and he didn't pitch for the Giants in a major league game until he was 18. After that year, he was sent to the Boston Red Sox where he was befriended by Ruth in 1919. That led to a long friendship with baseball's top celebrity. When Ruth went to the Yankees, Hoyt tried to go along.

"The surest way to become a winning pitcher," Hoyt theorized, "is to be on the same team with the Babe. Once he left the Red Sox, I went around insulting Boston officials so that they would trade me, preferably to the Yankees. Then the rest of those dumb guys could have the pleasure of pitching against the Babe."

Sure enough, Hoyt was traded to the Yankees and he went on to

Play-by-play announcer Waite Hoyt reads the Western Union report of a Reds game and then gives the description of the game over the Burger Beer Baseball Network.

become a big winner. He won 19 games his first year and beat the Giants twice in the 1921 World Series. He lost another, 1-0, on an error.

Hoyt went on to win 237 games, to become the only pitcher ever to beat the Reds on two consecutive Opening Days and to be elected to the Hall of Fame in 1969.

Still going strong at the age of 81, Hoyt is one of Cincinnati's most notable celebrities. But who knows what might have happened if he'd have played Larrupin' Lou in the movies 40 years ago?

The Youngest Pitcher Of Them All
JOE NUXHALL

It is unlikely that anyone as young as Joe Nuxhall will ever pitch in the major leagues again. He was a 15-year-old junior high school student from Hamilton, Ohio, a city about 25 miles north of Cincinnati, when he pitched his first game for the Cincinnati Reds in 1944.

The date was June 10. It was a hot, steamy afternoon at Crosley Field and the Reds were playing the St. Louis Cardinals — the mighty Cardinals who would go on to win the National League pennant.

America was at war and major league rosters were filled with players too old for military service, players who had a physical problem that prevented them from military service, or players who were too young to be drafted. Left-handed pitcher Joe Nuxhall, 15 years, 10 months, and 11 days old, was one of the youngsters.

Nuxhall was a sensation on the playgrounds in Hamilton. His fastball was fast. His curve ball was good. He was big for 15 years of age and he was better than any of the other kids in Hamilton.

He came to Cincinnati for a tryout. The Reds, needing fresh young players, signed him to a major league contract. But Joe never thought he would be used in a game. He figured he was just getting some experience on the big league level before he would be sent to the minor leagues.

How wrong he was.

"I thought Mr. McKechnie (manager Bill McKechnie) was kidding," Nuxhall said on the 30th anniversary of his first major league appearance. "But he wasn't."

It was the ninth inning and the game was hopelessly lost. The Reds were trailing, 12-0. It was time to take a look at that gangly kid from Hamilton.

"Warm up, Joe," McKechnie said. The manager had to repeat himself. Joe thought McKechnie was kidding. But the manager was serious and out to the bullpen trotted Nuxhall.

"I felt fine warming up on the sidelines," Nuxhall recalled. "It didn't get to me until I went out to the mound to start the ninth inning."

About 3,500 fans were on hand and they cheered when Nuxhall went onto the field to start the ninth. They cheered louder when he struck out the first batter. He walked the next man, then struck out the next. But it would take him some eight years to get his third out in the major league.

Before Nuxhall was removed, the Cardinals had scored five more runs. He walked five, hit a batter and allowed two hits as the Cardinals engineered the worst major league runaway, 18-0, since 1906.

Nuxhall doesn't remember what McKechnie said to him when he removed him from the game in favor of Harry Eisenhart. "I know he said something, but I was so numb emotionally I can't recall a thing," Nuxhall said.

The historic moment was not even mentioned in the next morning's paper. No headlines reported Nuxhall as the youngest player ever to pitch. The morning paper in Cincinnati simply stated, "Five Redleg hurlers served 'em up and ducked in the two hour and 23 minute clambake."

After that game, Nuxhall went to Birmingham and pitched only two-thirds of an inning there. It was a wasted year. He sat on bush-league benches in 1945 and dropped out of professional baseball in 1946, regaining his amateur status so he could play high school football and baseball at

Hamilton High School.

He came back to pro baseball in 1947 and then spent five years in such places as Muncie, Indiana, Tulsa, Oklahoma, and Charleston, West Virginia, before making it back to the major leagues in 1952 with the Reds.

He was with the Reds each year from 1952 until 1966 except 1961, missing his only shot at a World Series. He wound up with 135 victories and a lot of memories, but if he had it to do over again he would not have started nearly as young.

"If I were 15 again," Nuxhall said, "I would never sign a professional contract. Carry it beyond that: I wouldn't sign before I was certain I could complete a college education."

Nuxhall, however, has done well. Since retiring from the playing field, he has been the popular color commentator on the Reds radio network. He's also a familiar sight to early arrivals at Reds games: he's still pitching for the Reds — throwing batting practice nearly every day.

Major league baseball's youngest pitcher ever, 15-year-old Joe Nuxhall, gets advice from his manager Bill McKechnie.

The Whip That Cracked For A Season
EWELL BLACKWELL

For one season, Ewell Blackwell was baseball's best pitcher. His pitching accomplishments were hailed in 72-point type in newspaper headlines and were analyzed in in-depth magazine articles. He was the toast of the baseball world.

The year was 1947. This Cincinnati Reds right-hander looked like a sure Hall-of-Famer. He won 22 games, pitched one no-hitter and came within a whisker of duplicating Johnny Vander Meer's feat of two consecutive no-hit gems.

Blackwell was being compared to all the great pitchers. He won 16 consecutive games, a string topped only by Rube Marquard's 19 in a row for the New York Giants in 1912. He nearly dethroned Bob Feller as the major league strikeout king. He was being called the National League's "new Carl Hubbell, right-handed version."

The Reds had been waiting for such a season since the gangly, 6-foot-5-inch youngster had signed a small bonus contract with the club before the 1942 season. He was a phenomenon on the California sandlots, where he also played basketball and football. He starred on the same high school team as did Glenn Davis, the famous collegian who teamed with Doc Blanchard in the backfield at the United States Military Academy.

Blackwell had a buggy-whip motion; hence the nickname "The Whip." When he delivered a pitch to the plate, the ball was hard to follow. His big feet; his long, slender arms; his pretzel windup; his serpentine delivery and classic follow-through made Blackwell's sizzling fastball even harder to hit.

The Reds had to wait quite a while for his emergence as a star. Blackwell went straight to the major leagues in 1942 as a 21-year-old rookie. But he pitched in only two games before he was farmed to the Reds Class AAA team in Syracuse, New York. He burned that league up and certainly would have been a mainstay on the Reds staff in 1943, except that he went into the military service.

He returned from the service in 1946 and won only nine games, but manager Bill McKechnie had been eagerly anticipating his return. McKechnie, an astute observer of pitchers, told newspaper reporters that Blackwell would be "one of the truly great pitchers, one of the all-time greats."

The following season bore out McKechnie's prediction. Pulitzer-Prize-winning sports columnist Red Smith once described Blackwell as looking "like a fly rod with ears." Well, that "fly rod" posted a 22-8 record. During his marathon, 16-game winning streak, Blackwell pitched his no-hitter, a two-hitter and four three-hitters. He was removed for a pinch hitter only once during the streak.

The *pièce de résistance* was the no-hitter on June 18 against the Braves. Four days later, he nearly duplicated Vander Meer's double no-hit feat. Blackwell held Brooklyn hitless for $8\frac{1}{3}$ innings before Eddie Stanky singled up the middle, right between the pitcher's legs. Blackwell eventually settled for a two-hitter when Jackie Robinson also singled.

Waite Hoyt, a Hall-of-Fame pitcher for the Yankees and a radio broadcaster in Cincinnati who watched Blackwell pitch, was awed by Blackwell's ability.

"There was a time," Hoyt said, "when Blackie was as close to unbeatable as a pitcher can get. Yes, he could knock the bats out of their hands — and he did. I've seen him do it . . . . The right-handed hitters today can thank their lucky stars they don't have to hit against that string bean."

Unfortunately for Blackwell and the Reds, The Whip never came close to matching his 1947 record. He had arm problems in 1948 and his record dipped to 7-9. He had a kidney removed before the 1949 season and he was 5-5 that year.

By the mid-1950s, the pitcher, once compared to all the great ones of the past, was finished. The Reds sold him to the New York Yankees in 1952 and he finished up his career with the Yanks the next season.

Nevertheless, Ewell Blackwell will always be remembered for that one great season in 1947.

Right-handed pitcher Ewell Blackwell kisses the baseball after pitching a no-hitter against the Boston Braves on June 18, 1947.

The Man Who Broke A Barrier
CHUCK HARMON

It was a bright, chilly afternoon in Milwaukee on Saturday, April 17, 1954. The Cincinnati Reds were playing the Braves at Milwaukee County Stadium.

It was one of those typical early-season games—except for one thing. It marked the first time a black player appeared in a game for the Reds.

Chuck Harmon—a young, black infielder who had been a standout basketball player at Toledo University—went to the plate in the seventh inning to bat for Reds starting pitcher Corky Valentine. Although he popped up on the infield, it was a start, and his appearance blazed the trail in the Cincinnati organization.

Harmon's first appearance created little fanfare. In fact, in the game story in *The Cincinnati Enquirer* on April 18, the only mention of Harmon was that he batted for Valentine. In a sidebar story, a roundup of Reds notes, there was a brief mention, also, that Harmon had made his debut in the major leagues. But nowhere was anything said about this man breaking the color line for the Reds.

Seven years earlier, however, there was quite a fanfare when Jackie Robinson broke in with the Brooklyn Dodgers. Branch Rickey, the shrew general manager of the Dodgers, purchased Robinson's contract from Montreal in 1947, paving the way for many more black players to enter the major leagues. Soon most big-league teams were scouting the old Negro baseball leagues looking for players who could come immediately to the major leagues. There were plenty.

The Dodgers added Roy Campanella and Don Newcombe. Cleveland signed Larry Doby, the first black to play in the American League. Willie Mays, Hank Thompson and Monte Irvin went to the New York Giants. A new era was dawning in baseball.

After Harmon's arrival, more black players came to Cincinnati. In 1955 Joe Black, a former Rookie of the Year with the Dodgers, became the Reds first black pitcher.

Cincinnati's first black superstar was Frank Robinson. He was signed out of Oakland, California, by Bobby Mattick, who now is the manager of the Toronto Blue Jays. Robinson broke in sensationally with the Reds in 1956, winning the Rookie of the Year award. In 1961, when the Reds won the pennant, he received the Most Valuable Player accolade.

In the mid-1970s Robinson blazed a new trail: he was named manager of the Cleveland Indians, earning the distinction of being the first black manager in baseball history. Then, in 1981 at San Francisco, he became the first black manager in the National League.

Others followed Robinson to Cincinnati. Among them were Vada Pinson, a standout hitter throughout the 1960s, and Bobby Tolan, who played a key role in two pennants in the early 1970s.

Chuck Harmon, a native of Washington, Indiana, was the first black to appear in a game for the Reds. He batted behind Nino Escalera in the April 17, 1954, game.

The Strongest Man In Baseball
TED KLUSZEWSKI

If he had stayed with football, a professional career on the gridiron undoubtedly would have been in the offing.

If he had decided to stay with basketball, there would have been fewer stronger men fighting for rebounds.

But instead, Ted Kluszewski went for baseball and wound up one of the Cincinnati Reds greatest sluggers and a home-run hitter deluxe.

A left-handed hitter whose playing weight was near 240 pounds, Kluszewski was said to have the strength to hit a baseball out of any park in America — including Yellowstone.

"The first man to be killed by a batted ball will be an innocent stranger. He'll be minding his business, walking along Western Avenue behind Crosley Field. He'll be hit by a ball that was driven out of the park by Kluszewski," said National League umpire Larry Goetz.

He was considered the strongest man in baseball during the early and mid-1950s. He made a joke out of the 342-foot home-run barrier at Crosley Field. In 1954, when Kluszewski hit 49 home runs to lead the major leagues and set a team record, 34 of them soared over the right field fence at Crosley Field.

When talking about the strongest players in the game, Leo Durocher, manager of the New York Giants in the early 1950s, mentioned Gil Hodges of Brooklyn.

"What about Kluszewski?" he was asked.

"Kluszewski," Durocher retorted. "I'm talking about human beings."

When Kluszewski was at his best, he was as feared a hitter as Ted Williams, Stan Musial or other great ones.

"I do by brute strength," Kluszewski once explained, "what they do by finesse. I can hit a ball on the handle and give it a ride. Williams always gets the solid part of his bat on the ball. When a ball is pitched to me, I start my action early. That's why I look so bad when I'm fooled. Those wrist hitters can stop their action and resume. But once I start to swing, I'm dead."

Baseball was Kluszewski's third love in high school in Argos, Illinois. Football came first, then basketball.

He went to Indiana University on a football scholarship and made all-Big Ten his sophomore year, helping the Hoosiers win the conference championship.

It was in Bloomington, Indiana, home of IU, where the Reds first noticed the big first baseman. In order to avoid spring football practice, Kluszewski went out for the baseball team.

During the World War II years the Reds trained on the Indiana campus. Head groundskeeper Lenny Schwab first spotted this gentle giant who batted .429 as a Big Ten sophomore.

The Reds were reluctant to sign Kluszewski and end his college career prematurely since Indiana had loaned its facilities to the Reds for spring training. So an agreement was struck: When Klu wanted to turn professional, the Reds would then enter the bidding. That decision came in 1946 and Kluszewski became an instant sensation in the Cincinnati farm system. He batted .325 at Columbia, South Carolina, and .377 the next year at Memphis. He joined the Reds late that year and stayed with them until he was traded after the 1957 season.

Kluszewski is one of the few baseball players ever to hit at least 40 home runs in three consecutive

The bulging muscles of Ted Kluszewski could not be more pronounced as he visits with Reds owner Powel Crosley. Kluszewski made the sleeveless uniform fashionable.

years. He connected for 40 in 1953, 49 in 1954 and 47 in 1955.

Kluszewski's manager for four years (1954-57) thought Klu was one of the few players with a chance to break Babe Ruth's home-run record of 60 in a season.

"He'd break it," Birdie Tebbetts said in a 1955 *Saturday Evening Post* article, "if he played with the Giants in the Polo Grounds." The fence at the old park in Manhattan was less than 300 feet down the right field line.

But just at his peak, when many big years appeared ahead, Kluszewski, 32, was victimized by back problems. His home-run output in 1957 dropped to six, 29 less than the 35 he hit in 1956.

The Reds traded Klu in 1958, and he finished up his career with the expansion Los Angeles Angels in 1961.

Although he was a great power hitter, Kluszewski never struck out in great totals like some of his contemporaries. An average year resulted in about 30. When he hit 49 homers in 1954, that total was 15 more: 15 more homers than strikeouts. A more remarkable figure is his major league strikeout high: only 40.

Kluszewski won't make baseball's Hall of Fame. But for five years in his prime, he was about as good as any player who is in that Valhalla.

How A Home-Run Order Was Filled
SMOKY BURGESS

The speculation began midway through the 1956 season: Could the Cincinnati Reds break the National League record for most home runs in a season?

The 1948 New York Giants had established the record, hitting 221, but with such sluggers in the Cincinnati lineup as Ted Kluszewski, Gus Bell, Wally Post and a rookie named Frank Robinson, it appeared the Reds had a chance to catch the Giants.

As the season wore on, the Reds got closer and finally, on the last day of the season, they were within striking distance. Late in their final game against the Chicago Cubs at Wrigley Field, the Reds stood one short of tying the record.

Manager Birdie Tebbetts was aware of the record and looked down at Smoky Burgess sitting on the bench. He motioned for the substitute catcher to go to the plate as a pinch hitter. He told Burgess that he wanted a home run. Tebbetts' instructions were to swing from the heels, go for gusto, make it all or nothing. It was an unusual request because most of the time a manager will simply tell his pinch hitter to get his bat on the ball. Not this time with the record near at hand, though.

With that in mind, Burgess went to the plate.

"I remember it well," Smoky Burgess said not too long ago when he was in Cincinnati for a reunion of the 1956 team. "He told me to hit a home run."

And that's exactly what Burgess did. He sent a towering smash over the right field fence which became the record-tying round-tripper and the Reds went into the books alongside the Giants, both with 221 home runs.

"That was an unusual situation," Burgess added. "That was the only time I ever went to the plate in my entire career trying to hit a home run and actually doing it. Other times I went up trying to hit the ball out of the park, but I didn't do it then. That was the only time."

That home run was the seventh time that year he came off the bench to pinch-hit, but before his career was over, this left-handed hitter would make a name for himself as one of the game's best.

When he retired in 1967 after an 18-year career in the major leagues, Burgess was baseball's all-time leading pinch hitter, collecting 145 pinch-hits. That record has since been broken by Manny Mota.

Pitchers knew one thing when Old Smoke came lumbering up to the plate: he'd get his cuts. He wouldn't stand there and watch a lot of pitches go by.

He ended his career with the Chicago White Sox and they took advantage of his pinch-hitting ability. During his final three years, he went to the plate more than 200 times as a pinch hitter and came through 49 times. In both 1965 and 1966 he led the majors in total pinch-hits with 20 and 21.

Not all players can be good pinch hitters. It takes a special knack. And Smoky Burgess had it.

Smoky Burgess, a left-handed power hitter, blasted a pinch-hit home run on the final day of the 1956 season that enabled the Reds to tie the National League record for most homers in a season.

Center Field, Center Of Attention
GUS BELL

Before the Big Red Machine roared into Cincinnati and turned on the town like no other baseball team in the long and glittering history of the franchise, the most popular player quite possibly was Gus Bell, the hard-hitting outfielder who earned his cheers in the 1950s.

In many other eras, Gus Bell might have been the premier center fielder of his time, but he had unfortunate timing — playing when Willie Mays, Duke Snider and Mickey Mantle were plying their trade in New York.

Reds fans, however, considered Gus an equal to anyone and they cheered his performances. He was a dandy and performed magnificently for nine seasons for the Reds.

Born David Bell, he was a youngster playing baseball in his hometown of Louisville, Kentucky, when the nickname Gus was slapped on him. The young Bell was a catcher in those days. His cousin, a strong admirer of New York catcher Gus Mancusco, likened the little Bell boy to big-leaguer Gus. The nickname stuck and he forever after was known as Gus Bell.

Bell originally was signed by the Pittsburgh Pirates after a 1947 tryout in Indianapolis. He spent three seasons in the bush leagues — nearly quitting his rookie year when his batting average in Leesburg, Florida, was a meager .220. He arrived in the majors in 1950 as a Pittsburgh outfielder.

He played three years for the Pirates. Then came what he considered his big break: a trade to the Reds. He came under the tutelage of Rogers Hornsby, the Reds manager who is acknowledged as the best right-handed hitter of all time.

Bell had batted only .250 the year before his trade to the Reds and he admittedly was confused at the plate.

"He (Hornsby) straightened me out on things and showed me pointers about hitting that I'll never forget the rest of my baseball career," Bell told United Press before a spring game in 1954 in Lynchburg, Virginia.

"He said for me to aim everything through the box.

"Just try to knock the pitcher down. He said if I did that, I never would have a serious slump and that with my natural power, I'd get my share of home runs, too.

"Well," Bell continued, "I got 30 home runs and drove in 105 runs and had an even .300 batting average. Can't you see why I'm grateful to Hornsby?"

That was a great start and he endeared himself to the Cincinnati fans for the remainder of his career in the Queen City.

Bell's hitting was normally around the .300 mark. A long bout with blood poisoning took its toll in 1958 and he slumped to .252 that season.

As an outfielder, few rivaled Bell's skills. In 1959 he established a major league fielding record, playing 199 consecutive games without making an error.

"Gus is the most underrated outfielder in the league," Reds manager Birdie Tebbetts once said of Bell.

"Mays and Snider get the publicity, but for my money, Bell is their equal. He doesn't get his just due because he doesn't play in New York."

Bell played with the Reds through the 1961 season. When the National League expanded in 1962, he was picked by the New York Mets in the expansion draft. The Mets traded him to Milwaukee where he finished his career in 1964.

Today, Bell remains a great baseball fan and follows closely the American League box scores.

There's another Bell playing these days — David Gus Bell. He's known as Buddy, the son of Gus, and he's a chip off the old block. Except he's a third baseman.

Two of the greatest Reds center fielders ever, Gus Bell (left) and Edd Roush, played in much different eras as demonstrated by the contrast in their gloves.

A Swing Hitched To Stardom
FRANK ROBINSON

He had a hitch in his swing. He crowded the plate like few others ever had done. His arm went dead one year, and he couldn't play the outfield.

But that didn't prevent Frank Robinson from becoming one of the best players ever to put on the red-and-white Cincinnati uniform.

Robinson was a product of Oakland, California, and was first noticed by scouts at the age of 14 playing American Legion baseball. He had a big hitch in his swing then — just as he did when he terrorized National and American League pitchers.

"This kid has a hitch in his swing, but don't let anyone tamper with him. It's how he generates his power," Reds scout Bobby Mattick told Reds general manager Gabe Paul about Robinson. Mattick eventually signed him, hitch and all.

Robinson roared through the Cincinnati farm system, and in 1956 he was voted the National League Rookie of the Year. He smashed 38 home runs, tying the National League record for a rookie, a record he still shares with Wally Berger. Those 38 homers were tops for the club that year when it tied the National League mark.

Robinson's career at one point seemed to be short-lived. His right arm went dead, powerless. He couldn't throw. And ballplayers who can't throw are about as useless as automobiles without wheels. He was moved to first base. But after a season there, the arm came around. The only answer seemed to be that Robby had a sore arm, and a season of not throwing much let it heal.

Because Robinson crowded the plate — sometimes he actually leaned out over it — he continually was knocked down. But he seemed to thrive on it: many times he would get up out of the dirt and hit the next pitch over the fence. He was absolutely fearless at the plate and, regardless of how many times he was hit, he bounced right back up.

During Gene Mauch's reign as Philadelphia Phillies manager, he automatically fined any pitcher who knocked down Robinson $50 — quite a reversal for a manager known as one of the feistiest in the game.

Robinson played the outfield much the same way as he batted. He did not give in to fences and often crashed into an outfield wall on the dead run. When he played hard, there were few better at the game than Frank Robinson.

1961 was one of his finest years: he batted .321, hit 37 home runs and knocked in 124 runs. He led the Reds to their first pennant in 21 years and won the Most Valuable Player Award. Five years later he won the MVP again, but that time for the Baltimore Orioles.

It was after the 1965 season that Robinson was traded to Baltimore. Team-owner Bill DeWitt will never live down his statement that Robinson was "an old 30." But, at the time, the deal looked like a good one. Frank hadn't done much since his MVP year, and the Reds needed pitching, which they got.

Robinson's competitive spirit came home to haunt DeWitt and the Reds. He won the Triple Crown for the Orioles in 1966, and when he picked up his MVP trophy he laid claim to being the only player in baseball history to be named Most Valuable in both leagues.

In the early 1970s Robinson began setting his sights on managing. In 1975 he got his chance when Cleveland hired him as baseball's first black manager. Two years later he became the first black manager to be fired. He went on to Rochester in the minor leagues, then coached for Earl Weaver in Baltimore, and finally returned to managing in 1981 with the San Francisco Giants.

Robinson's career has been one of baseball's most unique. And one of the best. For that reason, he was ushered into the Hall of Fame last January — only the 13th player ever elected on the first ballot. Not bad for a kid who had a hitch in his swing.

The young Frank Robinson listens intently to manager Birdie Tebbetts prior to the 1957 season. His 38-homer rookie year in 1956 launched a Hall of Fame career.

The Man Who Managed To The End
FRED HUTCHINSON

The good die young. That cliché is probably as overworked a group of words as exists in the English language. Unfortunately, all too often it is the absolute truth.

A case in point: Fred Hutchinson. Former manager of the Reds. Dead at the age of 45. Cancer.

"How could a bug, no matter how vicious, destroy the living tissue of a body and mind as strong as Fred Hutchinson's when he should have been in the prime of his life?" Si Burick, sports editor of the *Dayton* (Ohio) *Daily News* asked in his column the day, November 12, 1964, Hutch died in Bradenton, Florida.

Everyone, foe and friend alike, asked that question. You see, Fred Hutchinson was a ballplayer's ballplayer, a manager's manager.

Hutchinson, one of the few former pitchers who went on to become a big league manager, was immensely popular in Cincinnati after he succeeded Mayo Smith in July 1959. Two years later, 1961, he guided the Reds to the National League pennant, surprising all the experts. During the next three years the Reds were contenders, losing once by three games and in 1964 by one game on the final day of the season.

Hutchinson managed the 1964 season knowing full well that cancer had a firm grip on his body and that he was dying. But he never gave in and seldom said anything about the terrible pain that consumed his body.

Twice he left the team for checkups and finally turned the club over to Dick Sisler the final two and one-half months, although Hutch would be in uniform at the park on his "good days."

Hutchinson had a famous temper, and even as he was dying, he spared nothing on an umpire if he thought the play was called wrong.

As a pitcher with Detroit, Hutch was known to take out his wrath on water coolers and light bulbs. He was more restrained as a manager, but there were times when he couldn't control himself. One night, after the Reds lost a close game to St. Louis on a ninth-inning home run, Hutch threw a bag of baseballs through his Crosley Field office window. Afterward he was a bit sheepish when he had to explain the hole in the window and the splintered glass to newsmen who descended on his office.

Another time, when the Reds lost a double-header to the New York Mets at the Polo Grounds, Hutch boiled. He sat by himself in the dugout for about half an hour. Finally he called the clubhouse and someone answered.

"Any so-called players still around?" Hutch asked. The clubhouse man said there still were a few remaining. "Get 'em out of there. I'm coming in."

It didn't take long for the place to empty. No one wanted to be around when Hutch roared in. He was mad — mad at himself, mad at the world, mad at the team. But he didn't want to say something or do something he later would regret.

Even though he had a hair-trigger temper, he had the complete respect of the men in the game — his own players, umpires, rival players and rival managers. He treated his players the way players thought they should be treated. At the same time, he could hold a strong rein on them. He was unique in that respect and that's what made him so great.

Hutch was a pitcher during his playing career. He once was a Minor League Player of the Year and went on to pitch for the Detroit Tigers.

When he played, he was just as fiery as a competitor as he was as a manager. But his bark often was much worse than his bite.

One particular evening Hutchinson had been roughed up early and knocked out of the game. He called his wife Patsy to come pick him up at Briggs Stadium in Detroit. Mrs. Hutchinson brought along young son Rick, who later would become an executive with the Milwaukee Brewers, but cautioned the youngster not to say anything to his father because of the poor outing that night. She mentioned something about Hutch getting his ears boxed off.

When Hutch got into the car, the young boy was curious. He looked his father over without saying a thing. Finally Hutch roared, asking the boy what was wrong.

"Mom said you got your ears boxed off, and I just wanted to see what they looked like," the boy said.

Naturally Hutch couldn't be mad, and they all had a good laugh, as did many of Hutch's players years later when the story was retold.

Reds manager Fred Hutchinson looks over a letter in the clubhouse during spring training in Tampa, Florida, in 1963. Hutch died of cancer the following year. He was the last person to wear Reds uniform No. 1.

Little League To Major League
JOEY JAY

Little Leaguers do grow up and, for a couple of seasons in the early 1960s, a former Connecticut Little Leaguer was a standout pitcher for the Cincinnati Reds.

Joey Jay, a right-hander, owns the distinction of being the first graduate of Little League baseball ever to play in the majors. Joey was 12 years old when the local league was established near his home in Middletown, Connecticut. Less than five years later he was in the major leagues, a 17-year-old bonus baby with the Milwaukee Braves.

Because he signed for a $40,000 bonus, Jay was forced to spend his first two professional seasons on the major league club. As a result, the raw but hard-throwing youngster saw little action. He appeared in only 18 games in the two years.

"That was a terrible rule, that bonus rule," Jay told *Sports Illustrated* writer Walter Bingham. "I got none of the experience I needed, and I took up a spot on the roster someone more deserving should have had. And what a drag I was on the ball club."

For a period of time during the 1950s, the major leagues invoked that bonus rule — a bonus player signed above a certain amount of money was required to stay in the majors for two years — as a way to try to keep down the payment of large bonuses to unproven kids.

Jay never made it big with the Milwaukee organization. After the 1960 season, when Jay had won only 24 games for the Braves in seven years, he was traded to the Reds along with Juan Pizarro for shortstop Roy McMillan.

The trade actually was a three-cornered deal. It also involved the Chicago White Sox. After the Reds had Pizarro, they then swapped him and pitcher Cal McLish to the White Sox for Gene Freese.

The acquisition of Jay and Freese, a hard-hitting, sometimes erratic third baseman, transformed the sixth-place Reds of 1960 into pennant contenders and winners in 1961.

"I contacted a couple of friends in the Milwaukee organization," manager Fred Hutchinson recalled in a 1961 *Sporting News* interview. "I was told that Jay had showed signs of maturing last year . . . that he was ready to realize the tremendous potential scouts had seen in him when the Braves signed him as a bonus player."

Jay was also highly touted by Bob Scheffing, the Detroit Tigers manager, who had been a coach at Milwaukee in 1960.

Said Scheffing, "I wanted to get Jay for the Tigers, but we had nothing to offer." Scheffing predicted in the spring of 1961 that Jay would "win more games than any other pitcher on the Reds pitching staff."

And that is what Joey Jay did. In fact, he won more games that year than any other pitcher in the National League — 21. He pitched four shutouts and became the first Cincinnati 20-game winner since Ewell Blackwell in 1947, the same year Jay was playing Little League ball back in Connecticut.

Jay was tough to deal with in contract negotiations after winning 21 in 1961. So he came up with a novel idea: He would buy up his contract and offer his services to any team in baseball because the Reds offer wasn't to his satisfaction.

He took his offer in the form of $250,000 to Cincinnati general manager Bill DeWitt. "You're out of your mind," DeWitt thundered. "I'm not in the business of selling contracts."

They then hammered out a new contract and a satisfied Jay went to work in 1962. Again he won 21 games and he was once more one of the top pitchers in the National League.

Always looking for the added edge on the mound, Jay came up with a couple of new pitches that made him effective. He called them the changeup screwball and the slip pitch. It was nothing new for Jay to experiment. When Milwaukee had optioned him to the minor leagues one year, he went to a sidearm and underhand delivery when all else failed.

Jay also came up with a pitching

delivery that was eventually ruled illegal. The idea was spawned one night in Los Angeles when the base-stealing Dodgers literally stole a game from the Reds.

"They beat us something like 3 to 1 or 3 to 2," Jay told *Sport Magazine* writer Roy McHugh. "And all three of their runs were the result of stolen bases, advancing an extra base on a hit, tagging up on a fly ball. I decided it wouldn't happen to me."

And it didn't. Pitching the next night, Jay varied his pitching motion with men on base. At times he went into a fast, abbreviated windup instead of the customary stretch. The stance he took on the mound, facing the batter with the ball in both hands at the belt buckle, kept the runner from knowing which move Jay intended to use.

The Dodgers stole no bases and Jay won his game. At the end of the season, the rules were changed and Jay's new pitching technique was outlawed.

The 1962 campaign was to be the last good one for Jay. He slumped to seven wins and 18 losses in 1963. In 1966 he was traded to the Atlanta Braves where he ended his major league career as he started it — in obscurity.

Right-handed pitcher Joey Jay works during an exhibition game in the early 1960s. Jay was a 20-game winner two years in a row for Cincinnati.

The Era Of The Dancing Knuckler
BOB PURKEY

August 16, 1961, is one of those "red-letter" dates in Cincinnati Reds history. It's a date that can be reflected upon, remembered, savored and called back to discussion from time to time.

To refresh some memories, here's what happened:

The Reds and the Los Angeles Dodgers were battling for the lead in the ever-tight National League pennant race. After Joey Jay had defeated Sandy Koufax the night before, the Dodgers held a one-game lead over Cincinnati.

The Reds and Dodgers were playing a double-header at the Los Angeles Coliseum, the Dodgers home park, before their lavish stadium in Chavez Ravine was constructed a couple of years later. More than 72,000 were in attendance and most expected a sweep by the Dodgers, possibly even the *coup de grâce* for Cincinnati. A double-header defeat for the Reds would have been a severe blow to their pennant chances.

But on the "night to remember" of August 16, it was Los Angeles that was knocked out of the pennant race.

The Reds swept both games. Bob Purkey, the knuckle-balling right-hander, fired a four-hit shutout in the opener, a 6-0 victory for Cincinnati. In the second game the Reds wasted little time getting four runs in the first inning and then romping 8-0 behind the sensational two-hit pitching by Jim O'Toole.

Cincinnati went in front by a game, the Dodgers were dead and the Reds went on to baffle the experts who had picked them as sixth-place finishers in a preseason poll. The Reds breezed to the pennant, winning by six games over the second-place Dodgers.

One of the big reasons for success that year was Purkey, who usually could be counted on to pitch a good game in a tight situation. When his knuckle ball danced, he was tough to hit. And unlike other pitchers who relied heavily on the knuckler, Purkey had other pitches he would use. His fastball was much better than adequate and he had a good slider as well.

"I don't have blazing speed," Purkey confirmed in a *Sporting News* interview in 1962, "but my fastball does move. And believe me, without it, I couldn't win."

In the strictest sense of the word, Purkey was a pitcher. Time and time he finessed a batter rather than overpowering him.

Purkey came to Cincinnati in one of the most one-sided trades the club ever made. After pitching for his hometown Pittsburgh Pirates for four seasons, he came to the Reds for left-hander Don Gross. In his seven seasons in Cincinnati, Purkey won 103 games and lost only 76. Gross won exactly six games for the Pirates and finally had to quit because of arm trouble.

Purkey won 16 games in the pennant-winning 1961 season, but his best year was in 1962. That year he was a strong Cy Young Award candidate when he won 23 games, lost only 5 and had a 2.81 earned run average. As good as that year was, it could have been much better with a few breaks.

He lost one game to the Chicago Cubs, 1-0. Another loss came 2-0 to Houston. In yet another outing against the Colt 45s, he pitched 10 scoreless innings in a game the Reds later won, 1-0, on Johnny Klippenstein's home run in the 13th inning.

Purkey pitched for the Reds until he was swapped to St. Louis in 1965. He went back to Pittsburgh the next year and, after working 10 games, he called it quits.

His major league record shows 129 victories. Most came with the Reds and the memories of his dancing knuckle ball remain fond in the minds of most Reds fans.

Pitcher Bob Purkey shows how he held the knuckle ball when he pitched for the Reds during the late 1950s and 1960s. Purkey won 23 games in 1963, his best year.

A Pen As Mighty As A Bat
JIM BROSNAN

In recent years it has become expectable for baseball players to write a book about their experiences on and off the baseball diamond.

Jim Bouton's *Ball Four* and Sparky Lyle's *The Bronx Zoo* were tales about the New York Yankees.

More than 20 years earlier, however, a Cincinnati pitcher penned a forerunner to many of today's sports books. Jim Brosnan shook up the baseball world in 1960 when his first book, *The Long Season,* a 75,000-word chronicle of the 1959 season, was published by Harpers.

"I was very naive," Brosnan said in an interview in 1976. "I was writing as a guy who liked to read and wrote it the way I would have liked to have seen it if I were picking it out to read.

"I wasn't aware I was breaking any taboos or attacking the establishment nor did I feel as if I was a social revolutionary."

One segment of Brosnan's first book was not too complimentary to the St. Louis Cardinals for whom Brosnan played part of the 1959 season until he was acquired by the Reds.

St. Louis manager Solly Hemus felt he was unjustly criticized and issued a steamy rebuttal to the "unhappy days" Brosnan wrote about.

Brosnan's first effort was a big hit with the book-buying public and he embarked on another. That one, less controversial, was a basic diary of the 1961 season when the Reds won the National League championship. Brosnan titled it *Pennant Race.* It, too, was a success, but Brosnan never made enough from his writing to give up his baseball career.

Brosnan grew up on Cincinnati's West Side, long a spawning ground for outstanding baseball players. He was a better hitter than pitcher in high school, but after he graduated from Xavier University in Cincinnati, the Chicago Cubs signed him as a pitcher.

He spent two full years with Chicago, 1955-56. Then, after working in eight games in 1957, he was dealt to the Cardinals.

After coming to Cincinnati in 1959, Brosnan was used almost exclusively as a relief pitcher. He made two early starts in 1960, was roughed up in both, and then went to the bullpen for the remainder of his major league days.

In 1961 when the Reds surprisingly won the pennant, Brosnan, a right-hander, formed a strong one-two combination with Bill Henry, a left-hander. They won 12 games between them, had 28 saves and appeared collectively in 100 games.

Early in the 1963 season, Brosnan was sold to the Chicago White Sox and after posting a 3-8 record for them, he retired.

If Brosnan's career as a baseball-playing writer disappointed anyone, it probably was his mother. She wanted him to become a doctor.

*Baseball pitcher-author Jim Brosnan sits in front
of his typewriter in 1962 as
he works on a book entitled Nine Innings.*

A Brief Stop At Second In '61
JIM BAUMER

One of the better trivia questions about the Cincinnati Reds goes something like this:

"Who was the Reds second baseman on Opening Day in 1961, the year the Reds won the pennant?"

Most answer that it was Don Blasingame. Wrong.

Blasingame didn't come to the Reds until April 27 in a trade for catcher Ed Bailey.

The player who started out that season of 1961 as the second baseman was Jim Baumer, who later went on to become general manager of the Milwaukee Brewers.

Baumer, signed originally by the Chicago White Sox, had an unusual career. He spent most of his playing days in the minor leagues and went 12 years between major league games.

Signed as a $50,000 bonus baby after high school graduation in Broken Arrow, Oklahoma, in 1949, Baumer appeared in eight games with the White Sox at the end of that season. His name didn't make it into another big league box score until Opening Day 1961, when he was listed as the No. 8 hitter for the Reds, starting at second base.

The Reds had traded Billy Martin to Cleveland and needed a second baseman. They got Baumer in the minor league draft before the start of the 1961 season, plucking him off the Salt Lake City roster.

He was never much of a minor league hitter, but he had a big year at Salt Lake City in 1960. He impressed scout Bobby Mattick, now the manager of the Toronto Blue Jays, and Dick Sisler, manager of the Reds Pacific Coast League farm team in Seattle. He batted .293 and hit 14 home runs in 1960. It looked like the Reds might be getting a real find.

"We would have invited him to train with us in '61 if Cincy hadn't drafted him," Pittsburgh Pirates general manager Joe Brown said. "He has versatility. You probably wouldn't call him great but he does everything well. We gave serious consideration to bring him up for our pennant drive (in 1960) when (Dick) Groat was injured."

From his start with the Reds, though, it was apparent Baumer would not hit much. General manager Bill DeWitt wanted a more steady and experienced second baseman. When Baumer had only three hits in his first 24 times at bat, he went to the bench. In late April, Blasingame came to the Reds and Bailey went to the San Francisco Giants. It was a deal the Reds could make because the Reds had several strong catchers.

Jim Baumer's career with the Reds lasted only 10 games and his tenth game in a Cincinnati uniform was his last in big league baseball.

Both Jim Baumer and Don Blasingame are still in baseball today. The Philadelphia Phillies are prospering from Baumer's front-office expertise. He is director of Minor Leagues and Scouting for the Phils, and under his direction they have put together one of the strongest farm systems in professional baseball.

Blasingame's current participation in baseball is literally a world apart: he manages a professional team in Japan. The Blazer went to the Orient in the mid-1960s to play for the Nankai Hawks in Osaka, Japan. After a couple of seasons, he joined the coaching staff and in 1970 was named the team's manager—or as they call it in Japan, head coach. He is the only American ever to hold that high position in Japanese baseball.

Don Blasingame replaced Jim Baumer at second base in late April 1961, after being acquired from the San Francisco Giants. He appeared in 122 games for the Reds that year.

Jim Baumer, the starting second baseman on Opening Day in 1961, takes a practice swing at Crosley Field. Baumer played little that year and lost his job to Don Blasingame.

Man's Best Friend
TONY PEREZ

They called him "Dog" or "Doggie."

Not as in, "man, he's a real dog," or "man, he really dogs it."

He was known as Dog as in, "man's best friend."

If not man's best friend, Tony Perez certainly was the Cincinnati Reds best friend during a standout career from 1965 through 1976.

Tony Perez was a popular favorite of the fans when he played in Cincinnati. An even-tempered, always-smiling big Cuban, Perez earned the fans' love with his ability to get runners home.

"If the game goes long enough," said Dave Bristol, the Reds manager from 1967 through 1969, "Tony Perez will find a way to win it." And many, many times he did. For 11 consecutive years he batted-in at least 90 runs each season, and in one nine-year stretch he averaged 104 RBI. Much of that time he was batting behind Johnny Bench who led the National League three different times in RBI during the 1970s.

Perez was a genuine superstar when he played in Cincinnati, but for some unexplainable reason he ranked behind Bench, Pete Rose and Joe Morgan. Perhaps Bench summed up Perez's demeanor and easy-going manner best when talking one day about the Reds publications which featured pictures of the top players.

"They've got me on the cover of the media guide," Bench said. "They've got Pete on the scorebook and Joe on the yearbook. And Tony . . . he really doesn't care."

While Bench, Morgan and Rose all competed for "ink" in their own ways, Perez sat back and watched. He said it never bothered him.

"It was tough in the beginning," Tony said. "But I didn't care. Rose is big, then Bench and Morgan. Am I jealous? No, it never hurt my feelings.

"Whatever the fans think, I never think of myself as fourth or as any number."

Asked once how he thought of himself, his answer was consistent with his stylish manner.

"Just happy to be part of baseball," Tony said. "And proud. Proud of my runs batted in. And because I think I do my job. It was never important to me to be number one."

While he may have played fourth fiddle in some respects, there was no doubt how his teammates felt about him.

"With a man in scoring position, and two out, whom would I want up there?" Rose asked himself. "Perez."

"More than anybody else on the team?" he was asked.

"More than anybody else in baseball," Rose replied.

"More than yourself?"

"More than myself."

Indeed, that is high praise.

Tony Perez will long be remembered for many home runs and many runs batted in with the Reds, but the three home runs he hit during the 1975 World Series stand out in a big way.

He went into Game No. 5 hitless in 15 times at the plate. But suddenly, the sure out in the middle of the Reds lineup blasted two big shots out of the park.

"He finally joined the people he belongs with," wrote Jim Murray, the nationally syndicated columnist from Los Angeles, "the Ruths, Gehrigs, Mantles, Berras . . ."

Then in the seventh game he hit his biggest. The Reds had blown Game No. 6 and, after a couple of innings of Game No. 7, it looked like Boston would win the World Series.

But in the fifth inning with a man on base, Perez got the Reds back into contention. Down 3-0 at the time, Perez wasn't fooled by Bill Lee's bloop ball. Instead, he jumped all over it, rifling a shot over Fenway Park's Green Monster in left center field. The Reds were on the way back thanks to Perez, and they went on to win the game in the ninth inning.

After the 1976 World Series it was time for the Reds to make a decision. Danny Driessen, a young infielder, was challenging for a chance to play. By now Perez was 35 years old and the Reds couldn't guarantee him he would play regularly in 1977. So he gave his approval and the Reds traded Tony to the Montreal Expos. He had three good years there and then moved on to the Boston Red Sox.

When Perez returned to Cincinnati for the first time as a member of the Expos, he was given a five-minute standing ovation. There was no doubt for what his nickname stood.

To some, Tony Perez may have been the fourth wheel on the Big Red Machine, but his peers knew him as a great clutch RBI man.

When Hustle Won An All-Star Game
PETE ROSE

Pete Rose will be remembered in a variety of ways by Cincinnati Reds faithfuls.

The first impression he made as a young player in 1963 was sprinting to first base on a walk. That earned Rose the nickname "Charlie Hustle," which was applied to him by New York Yankees pitcher Whitey Ford.

He will be remembered as baseball's first $100,000 singles hitter, then later as a jet-setting free agent, offering his services to anyone who would listen to his multimillion-dollar talk.

No one will ever forget the 1973 Championship Series at Shea Stadium in New York when he started a fight with Mets shortstop Bud Harrelson. Rose remarked later, "Who else could knock the Egypt-Israeli war off page 1 in New York?"

Then there was 1978 when Rose's name was in headlines all year. First, he collected his 3,000th career hit on May 5 against Montreal. Later he put together the longest batting streak in modern National League history, hitting safely in 44 consecutive games.

But if there is any one incident that spells out exactly how this Cincinnati native has played throughout his career, it is the 1970 All-Star game, played ironically enough at Riverfront Stadium in Cincinnati.

The situation in the All-Star game was this:

The score was tied, 4-4, and two men were out in the bottom of the 12th inning. It was a hot, muggy night along the Ohio River and the crowd was getting restless, wanting something to happen.

Rose was on second base. Chicago's Jim Hickman was at the plate facing California left-hander Clyde Wright. Hickman lined a pitch up the middle and Rose headed for home plate.

"I could hear Leo (third base coach Leo Durocher) holler 'you gotta go, you gotta go,'" Rose recalled later.

Indeed, Pete went. As he approached the plate Rose realized that catcher Ray Fosse, the backstop from Cleveland, had the plate blocked.

"All I could see when I went in there was this big mountain," Rose said.

Normally, when Rose slides, he slides head-first, but a head-first slide in this situation might have decapitated him. So he took a different route.

"I had to try to hit his glove and reach in," Rose remembered. "He was about two feet in front of the plate. All I could see were those shin guards. If I slid in there, I could have broken both legs."

So Pete lowered his head and left shoulder and went into Fosse. Splat. When they picked up Ray Fosse, the game was over. Rose had scored and the National League had won, 5-4.

Both were banged up. Rose slightly injured his left thigh. Fosse had a more severely bruised right shoulder.

The play drew sharp criticism from some. How could Rose play this game as if it were the seventh game of the World Series, some asked?

"I didn't particularly like the play," California shortstop Jim Fregosi said.

"Who knows? Maybe he should have run around me," Fosse said.

But Rose doesn't play that way and people should have realized that fact. He plays the game like a little boy, always going full tilt. There was nothing untypical about Rose's All-Star performance. Anyone who had watched Pete Rose play very much would have been disappointed had Charlie Hustle met the obstacle at the plate any other way.

Rose has gone on to enjoy many great years. During the 1981 season, he moved past Stan Musial and became the all-time hit leader in National League History.
His All-Star opponent at the plate in 1970, Fosse, never seemed quite the same player after that collision and he never again became an All-Star.

In this sequence of photos, Pete Rose has crashed into American League catcher Ray Fosse to score the winning run in the 1970 All-Star game at Riverfront Stadium.

"Some Kind Of Man" And Manager
SPARKY ANDERSON

It was "Sparky Who?" in October 1969 when the Cincinnati Reds hired George Anderson to become the 44th manager in the history of the club. But by October 1970 everyone knew Sparky Anderson after he led Cincinnati to the Western Division crown and the National League pennant.

Sparky, however, took little credit for the success, preferring to give his players their due. "Eleven other managers in our league could have won 102 games with these players," Anderson said.

Catcher Johnny Bench, who won the Most Valuable Player Award that year, thought differently though.

"Something happened last spring," Bench said after the 1970 Series. "We knew we had a good ball club, but something happened. It was Sparky Anderson. We call him John, as in John McGraw."

That good start was only an omen of better things to come. Before he was fired after the 1978 season, Anderson established a Cincinnati record that may never be broken. He won 863 games to become the winningest skipper in club history. His teams won five Western Division championships, four National League pennants and back-to-back world titles in 1975 and 1976.

Except for 1959 when Anderson was the starting second baseman for the Philadelphia Phillies and one other season when he was a San Diego coach, he spent 16 years in the minor leagues before being selected as the Reds manager.

After quitting as a player, he took a cue from former Reds manager Charles Dressen and began managing in the minor leagues. Starting with Toronto. He was fired after his team finished fifth, and he switched to the Cardinals farm system in 1965 where he came under the influence of Bob Howsam, then the St. Louis general manager.

Howsam brought Anderson with him in 1968 to the Cincinnati organization, installing him as the manager at Asheville, North Carolina, in the Class AA Southern League.

One year later Sparky was coaching third base for the San Diego Padres, and Howsam was getting impatient with Dave Bristol, who couldn't get the Reds over the hump and into a division championship. When Cincinnati finished third in 1969, a call went out for Anderson to come to Cincinnati.

From the very beginning Sparky made quite an impression. His even-tempered personality tended at times to cloud a perpetual inner drive. "There are some people who would rather follow," said Sparky. "but me, I'd rather lead. There isn't any shortcut to success, it just takes plenty of hard work."

Sparky gained national attention — and respect — after the 1970 World Series. He refused to dispute umpire Ken Burkhardt's call of a controversial collision at home plate. Burkhardt was in the wrong position to make the call, but Sparky didn't make an issue out of it.

Later in that same Series he impressed NBC's Joe Garagiola, who was telecasting the game. That situation involved Sparky's use of reserve catcher Pat Corrales in the fifth game. Sparky sent the seldom-used Corrales to the plate in the ninth inning in place of Hal McRae, a much better hitter.

"Why?" Sparky said, when asked his reason for doing that. "This Series is the dream of every man in baseball. He came thousands of miles for this and he may never get this close again. I think there will be more for him, but I couldn't forget him."

Garagiola, himself a former participant in the World Series, was shocked and impressed. "Here's a man with troubles. But here, one of the big moments of his life, he forgets his own problems to consider the feelings of another human being. That takes some kind of man."

There's no question, Sparky Anderson is some kind of man. And Reds baseball history is much richer because of him.

Sparky Anderson, winningest manager in Reds history, protests a call to umpire Ed Vargo during a game at Riverfront Stadium.

Five Gold Gloves At Short
DAVE CONCEPCION

For a guy who in his first two seasons as a regular shortstop in the Reds starting lineup batted .205 and .209, Dave Concepcion has come a long way.

He has come such a long way that when he finally decides at the end of this decade that he has had enough, they just might have to clear some space for him in Cooperstown. He certainly has all the earmarks of the Hall of Fame's next shortstop.

Concepcion has developed into one of baseball's best all-round players. His tremendous range and strong arm have earned him five Gold Gloves, symbolic of defensive greatness. After the slow start at the plate, his composite batting average in the following nine seasons, from 1973 through 1981, was .281, and twice he hit over .300. When he batted .300 in 1978, he became the first Reds shortstop in more than 50 years to do so.

He can run bases, too. Entering the 1982 season, Concepcion had stolen 236 bases with a high of 41 in 1974. And he has been named to the National League All-Star team eight times.

"George Foster has a lot more power," said Houston Astros manager Bill Virdon, "but if there's a runner in scoring position and the Reds need only one run, then Concepcion's the guy I don't want to see up there at the plate.

"Pee Wee Reese, Alvin Dark, Roy McMillan and Dick Groat were among the best I've seen, but for all-round ability, especially range, I can't put any of them ahead of Concepcion."

David Ismael Concepcion was a skinny, 19-year-old kid from Venezuela when the Reds signed him in 1967. There was no questions that he could "pick it." That's the way baseball players describe superb defense. But Virgilio Mata, another Venezuelan shortstop, signed at the same time with Concepcion, and Mata appeared to be much further advanced. It seemed in the beginning that Mata would be the real plum.

Mata, however, peaked somewhere at about the Class AA level in the minor leagues. Concepcion kept improving, and by 1970 he was in the major leagues. He shared the shortstop position that year with Woody Woodward on the National League pennant-winning team.

Although Concepcion hit .341 in a part-season at Class AAA Indianapolis and then .260 playing part-time in his rookie National League season, his bat didn't scare anyone in 1971 when he won the starting job with the Reds. He hit only .205 that season, then followed it with a .209 average in 1972. But his defensive prowess made people overlook his problems at the plate.

It was in the following year, 1973, that his bat came alive, too, and it has been cooking ever since. Davey batted .287 in 1973 and was named to the All-Star team. Two days before the All-Star game, however, he suffered a broken ankle and missed the remainder of the season.

The big question remained: would he have the mobility to play shortstop after the injury? The answer was a resounding yes.

Concepcion came back in a big way. He played with reckless abandon in 1974. He stole 41 bases in 44 tries. He batted .281. And he won his first of five Gold Gloves.

Through the years Reds fans have always liked their shortstops. The first great one was George Wright on the 1869 Red Stockings. He was considered the best baseball player of his time. In the late 1890s and early 1900s, Tommy Corcoran was a favorite.

Larry Kopf, Hod Ford, Leo Durocher, Billy Meyers and Eddie Miller followed. Then came Roy McMillan in 1951. He was acknowledged as the best the Reds had ever had.

But Concepcion has replaced McMillan at the top of the list. He was the best shortstop in baseball during the 1970s. And someday he will sit alongside some of the other great ones in the Hall of Fame.

Agility and quickness help Dave Concepcion make the tough plays expected of a five-time Gold Glove winner.

The Occasional Home-Run Hitter
HAL KING

Hal King was a paunchy, left-handed hitter who played for the Cincinnati Reds in 1973 and 1974. He was a catcher, but comparing him to Johnny Bench would be like comparing the sun and the moon. King was a major league player for parts of seven seasons for one primary reason, and only one primary reason. Occasionally he could hit a home run.

He hit only 24 in his career and if he hadn't connected on a hot summer afternoon against the Los Angeles Dodgers, King probably would never be remembered as having played for the Reds. But he had one great day in the sun and because of it, the Reds made a miracle comeback and won the National League's Western Division title in 1973.

The day was July 1, 1973, and the Dodgers owned a whopping 10-game lead over Cincinnati. The dreaded guys from out West already had won the first two games of this important series and suddenly were starting to count their pennant money. Until, that is, hero Hal King came to the plate in the ninth inning of the first game of the Sunday afternoon double-header.

Don Sutton, the ace of the Los Angeles staff and the holder of almost every career Dodgers pitching record, had kept the Reds off balance all afternoon. Los Angeles took a 3-1 lead to the bottom of the ninth and it looked like the Reds would fall 11 games behind and virtually out of the pennant race.

The Reds had a man on with two outs; then Sutton walked Bench. Manager Sparky Anderson sent King to the plate as a pinch hitter, but it's doubtful anyone in the park figured the Reds had much of a chance. It was the Dodgers best pitcher against a guy hitting .180.

Sutton worked the count to 2-2 and seemed to have King set up for a strikeout. All of a sudden the game and the entire season turned around. Sutton hung a screwball up in King's eyes and King rifled the pitch over the right-field fence. It was a three-run homer, the Reds won the game, 4-3, and the big comeback was on.

The Reds won the second game that afternoon and beat the Dodgers again the next night. By early September Cincinnati had caught up, and by the end of the month the Reds had snatched the division championship out of Los Angeles' hands.

"I was looking for a fastball, I mean I hadn't seen a pitch all day coming off the bench," King said after the game. "He tricked me. Didn't throw me one fastball."

Hal King was one of those swing-from-the-heels hitters and that's exactly what he did when he faced Sutton. He swung so hard, in fact, that he tore his shoes.

King had a unique year for the Reds in 1973. He had only eight hits and four of them were home runs, three coming off the bench. He went to the plate with one thing in mind: home run.

Hal King's major league career spanned 1967 through 1974, but only in 1970 with Atlanta did he bat as many as 200 times in a season. He wasn't a robust hitter, owning only a .214 lifetime mark.

But for one afternoon he was more than Hal King. He was Cincinnati King as the city toasted him as the guy who turned the 1973 baseball season around.

Reserve catcher Hal King will always be remembered for his pinch-hit home run against the Dodgers in 1973.

The Slugging Second Sackers
KAMPOURIS/MORGAN

The two most prolific home-run-hitting second basemen in the history of the Cincinnati Reds are a pair of little dynamos, weighing no more than 160 pounds and standing no taller than 5 feet, 8 inches.

Until Joe Morgan came along and established a new record in 1973, the Cincinnati mark for most season homers by a second baseman belonged to a fellow they called the Galloping Greek.

He was Alex Kampouris, a right-handed hitter who made his mark at the age of 24. He then became a virtual unknown the remainder of his career in the major leagues.

Kampouris, a product of the Class AAA Pacific Coast League's Sacramento club, hit 17 home runs in 1937 and seemed on the verge of becoming one of baseball's big names.

But he couldn't hit for a high average and Kampouris lasted only parts of nine years in the big leagues, hitting only 45 lifetime major league home runs.

When Kampouris set the Reds record of 17 in 1937, he improved his home-run total by an even dozen over the previous year.

When he wasn't hitting the ball over the fence, however, he often was striking out. He batted only .249 that season, not much in an era that featured a lot of high batting averages.

Kampouris played three full years with the Reds. In 1938 he was sent to the New York Giants in a trade for Wally Berger, the veteran outfielder who was also known for his home-run-hitting prowess. The deal proved to be valuable for the Reds because Berger was a big help in 1939 when the Reds won their first of two consecutive pennants.

Kampouris spent 1940 in the minor leagues and was out of the big leagues for good in 1944.

The Reds had many other fine second basemen after Kampouris — Lonnie Frey, Bobby Adams, Johnny Temple and even Pete Rose. None were home-run hitters until Morgan joined the Reds in a trade from the Houston Astros after the 1971 season.

Morgan, a left-handed hitter with a powerful swing, had hit as many as 15 home runs in a season with Houston. That was a remarkably high figure since he played half his games in the Astrodome, well-known as a home-run-hitter's nightmare because the flight of the ball does not carry as well indoors as it does outdoors.

Joe hit 16 home runs in 1972, his first year with the Reds, and nearly broke Kampouris'

long-standing record. It seemed like only a matter of time before Morgan would be known as the best home-run-hitting second baseman in Reds history.

Morgan went into the record books in 1973 when he raked National League pitching for 26 home runs. Joe shot past Kampouris' record in August as he blossomed into a power-hitter deluxe.

But Morgan wasn't finished with his assault on the Reds record book. A better year was yet to come. That year came in 1976 when he won his second straight National League Most Valuable Player Award.

Batting third on Cincinnati's power-laden World Championship team, Morgan hit 27 home runs, leaving a mark that is unlikely to be topped for years to come.

If Alex Kampouris was the virtual epitome of the flash-in-the-pan, Joe Morgan was the opposite: Indeed, a great Reds home-run hitter.

Alex Kampouris was a home-run-hitting second baseman. He held the Reds record with 17 in 1937 until Joe Morgan broke it in 1973.

Joe Morgan receives the National League Most Valuable Player Award during ceremonies at Riverfront Stadium in 1976.

A Catcher's Hit That Wasn't Caught
JOHNNY BENCH

It was a grey, dreary October afternoon in 1972 at Riverfront Stadium in Cincinnati. The situation for the Cincinnati Reds looked even gloomier than the weather. The team was just about out of time in its quest for the National League pennant.

The fifth game of the National League's Championship Series saw Pittsburgh leading, 3-2, in the ninth inning. All the Pirates had to do was retire the Reds without a score and the pennant would fly in the Steel City instead of in Cincinnati. What transpired, however, turned out to be one of the most disastrous innings in the history of the Pittsburgh franchise.

Dave Giusti, a veteran relief pitcher who specialized in an off-speed pitch called a palm ball, had come on for the Pirates to protect their slim lead. The first batter he faced in the ninth was Johnny Bench.

The two had faced each other many times. Bench knew Giusti would try to get him with a palm ball, a pitch that comes to the plate looking like a fastball, but much slower. And Giusti knew he had to keep his pitch away from Bench's power area.

Bench quickly got in the hole with two strikes, but not before bringing the crowd of 41,887 to its feet with a 400-foot shot to left field that was foul by about 20 feet. The ball's path looked like a game-tying home run, but then it hooked considerably foul.

The crowd realized that when a batter comes that close to a home run, that's usually it and he's finished. And Giusti knew he had Bench where he wanted him, one ball and two strikes.

Pittsburgh's pitcher delivered a palm ball away from Bench and out of his power zone, a bit high and outside. Bench measured the speed correctly and didn't try to pull the pitch to left field. Uncharacteristically, Bench went with the pitch, met it squarely and hit a long fly to right field. Pittsburgh right-fielder Roberto Clemente went back to the right center-field fence. He would have needed to have been 12 feet tall to catch the ball.

The ball rocketed over the fence at about the 375-foot marker. It was a game-tying home run. The crowd went wild, the Reds dugout erupted and suddenly the game was tied and Pittsburgh didn't have a lock on the pennant.

It was a big ninth inning. Tony Perez and Denis Menke singled. George Foster ran for Perez and went to third base when Cesar Geronimo hit a long fly ball to right.

Bob Moose now was on to pitch for the Pirates and Hal McRae was at the plate as a pinch hitter. Moose fired his second pitch to McRae in the dirt. It eluded catcher Manny Sanguillen, went to the backstop and Foster scampered home with the pennant-winning run.

That home run by Bench was the only home run that he hit in the 1972 Championship Series, but he connected with considerable frequency throughout that regular season and for his entire career. In 1972, as he was in 1970, Bench was the major league home-run king, hitting 40 in 1972 and 45 in 1970.

In his career Bench has hit 356 homers, 30th on the all-time baseball list when the 1981 season opened. More impressively, Bench has hit more home runs than any catcher in the long history of the game, 356.

Bench passed Yogi Berra in 1980 when he ran his total as a catcher to 323, 10 more than the mark Berra established. The remainder of Bench's total came when he played first base, third base, the outfield or was sent to the plate as a pinch hitter.

When Bench decides to retire, he should have to wait only the mandatory five years before he is inducted into baseball's Hall of Fame. He should be a certain first-ballot pick.

Few would disagree that Johnny Bench is the best catcher ever to put on the equipment.

Johnny Bench with this swing hit a lead-off home run in the ninth inning to tie the final game in the 1972 League Championship Series against Pittsburgh.

The Best World Series Ever Played
GAME NO. 7 -- 1975

The Reds have been involved in the World Series eight different times, but none was as exciting as the 1975 seven-game affair with the Boston Red Sox. By many who watched and reported, it was called "the best World Series ever played."

It had everything — controversial calls, fine defense, clutch hitting, tight pitching, 11th-hour heroes and plenty of Hollywood scriptlike drama.

The Reds owned a 3-2 advantage after five games. The first two games were played in Boston's Fenway Park and the next three were played at Cincinnati's Riverfront Stadium.

When the two teams returned to Boston to finish up the Series, it rained and rained and rained. Three straight days the games were rained out and nearly a week went by without Game No. 6 being played. But that failed to dent the enthusiasm one iota.

It looked like the Reds would win in six games. They held a comfortable three-run lead late in the game, but Bernie Carbo, who had played on Cincinnati's 1970 pennant-winner and who was runner-up in Rookie of the Year balloting that season, came off the bench to hit a three-run homer and tie the game.

The two teams battled into extra innings. Finally, in the 12th, the Sox won. Boston catcher Carlton Fisk sent the Boston fans home happy. He hit a leadoff homer off Pat Darcy to give the Red Sox a 7-6 victory. The memory of his standing at home plate, using body English to keep the ball fair, then throwing up his hands as the ball went over the Green Monster — Boston's big left field wall — remains intact in many a fan's mind.

Boston had not won a World Series since 1918 but on October 22, 1975, there wasn't a Red Sox fan anywhere who was doubting the drought had been broken. It looked like the Red Sox had the Reds where they wanted them, and it seemed it would be the Reds who would be World Series winless for the fourth straight time.

The Red Sox hopes were reinforced early in Game No. 7 when Boston took a quick 3-0 lead off Don Gullett, Cincinnati's top left-hander, and knocked him out of the game. Jack Billingham came on, though, and gave the Reds a chance.

In the fifth inning with the Reds still trailing 3-0, Tony Perez got two runs back. Bill Lee, the Boston starter, threw Perez a slow ball, a pitch that Lee called his "Leephus" pitch. It was a takeoff on Rip Sewell's Eephus, a blooper that comes to the plate somewhat like a slow-pitch softball does. Perez wasn't fooled and cracked a two-run homer. It was suddenly 3-2 and the Reds were starting to rumble.

Pete Rose singled home a run in the top of the seventh to tie the game. The tide had turned. Boston couldn't score and the Reds were on the move. In the ninth, rookie Boston pitcher Jim Burton faced left-handed-hitting Joe Morgan. Rose was on second base. Morgan grounded a single up the middle, Rose scored and all the Reds had to do was hold the Sox.

That chore was entrusted to Will McEnaney, a young left-hander who had teamed with Rawly Eastwick all season long to give the Reds baseball's best bullpen. He got two easy outs, then faced Carl Yastrzemski, Boston's aging superstar. Yaz couldn't handle McEnaney's offering. He lofted a short fly to center field. It was no problem for Cesar Geronimo. Seemingly before he caught the ball, McEnaney had leaped into the arms of catcher Johnny Bench.

The Reds had won the World Series and a wait of 35 years finally was over.

A jubilant Will McEnaney and Tony Perez celebrate the Reds victory over Boston in the 1975 World Series, arguably the greatest Series in baseball history.

The Man Is Terrific
TOM SEAVER

Tom Seaver was one of the greatest power pitchers in the history of baseball. In the last few years, however, when age has eroded some of that power, Seaver has become a finesse pitcher — an artistic hurler who uses years of experience to continue to excel.

In Seaver's opinion, the transition from power to finesse is not something that happens overnight. Even early in his career he began thinking of not relying solely on his great fastball. As he explained, "It is an overall preparation through your entire career when you experiment with different pitches, different grips, and different ways to move the ball. It has been a gradual transition."

He has also become the ultimate thinking man's pitcher. He knows exactly how he will pitch to each hitter, then he does it.

"It's just a matter of odds," Seaver said, "where I feel my best odds are to get out of an inning. The decision process is probably the most enjoyable, regardless of what the decision is. It's intriguing — the understanding and the evaluation that lead to the solution of the problem."

At times he pitches like he's in the midst of a card game. Take, for instance, a game in 1981 against the San Francisco Giants. The game was scoreless in the bottom of the ninth, and the Giants had runners on first and third. Seaver suggested to Reds manager John McNamara that he make the somewhat unorthodox move of walking Milt May. Cold calculation told Seaver that Johnnie LeMaster was the out he was looking for.

"That ninth inning was like playing bridge," Seaver said after he won the game, 1-0, in the 10th inning. "How are you going to play it? Where do your best chances lie? It was fun. It was the kind of thing that's rewarding for me as a pitcher."

Seaver did not lose that time, nor has he lost often in a remarkable career that probably will lead him to a first-ballot election to the Hall of Fame a few years hence.

Seaver spent the early part of his career with the New York Mets. He won three Cy Young Awards and was generally recognized as the best pitcher in baseball. But on June 15, 1977, in a blockbuster trade, the Reds acquired him for four players. Since joining the Reds, Seaver has reached several memorable milestones.

The first came a year and a day after the trade. It was a no-hitter. Three times previously Seaver had taken a no-hitter into the ninth inning only to come away empty. This time, against the St. Louis Cardinals, he prevailed.

He did it without much of a fastball, but his curve was brilliant. "I always felt that if I ever pitched a no-hitter," Seaver said, "that it would come on a night like this, on a night when I wasn't over-powering."

The 1981 season saw Seaver overcome two more barriers, two which few pitchers have even come close to.

First came his 3,000th strikeout. On April 18, St. Louis' Keith Hernandez swung and missed a high slider, and Seaver became only the fifth player in history to reach 3,000.

Then on May 20 in Chicago, Seaver joined the exclusive 250-victory club. Before the season was finished, he raised his total to 259, 28th on the all-time list.

Seaver had one of his poorest seasons ever in 1980, winning only 10 and losing eight. His ERA ballooned to 3.64. His shoulder was bothering him. Finally, for the first time in his career, he went on the disabled list with a serious arm problem.

Rest sometimes does magical things to pitching arms. When Seaver returned late in the season, he won six of seven decisions. Add that to a 14-2 record in 1981, and Seaver posted a 20-3 record following his trip to the DL.

How long can Tom Terrific pitch? Probably long enough to get 300 victories. Remember Warren Spahn? His fastball was washed up when he was 41 years old, but he won 21 games. Tom Seaver appears capable of doing the same.

With his distinctive style, Tom Seaver uncorks another pitch en route to more than 3,000 strikeouts and 250 wins.

INDEX

A

Aaron, Hank: 16
Adams, Bobby: 8,142
Alexander, Grover Cleveland: 92
Allen, Ethan: 60,61
Allison, Douglass: 23
Anderson, Sparky: 9,84,136,137,140
Anson, Cap: 26

B

Baker, Bill: 100
Baker, Del: 87
Bancroft, Dave: 66
Bartell, Dick: 102
Baumer, Jim: 130,131
Beggs, Joe: 104,105
Bell, Buddy: 118
Bell, Gus: 116,118,119
Bench, Johnny: 9,16,132,136,144,145,146
Berger, Wally: 120,142
Berra, Yogi: 96,144
Bescher, Bob: 42,43,71
Billingham, Jack: 146
Black, Joe: 112
Blackwell, Ewell: 110,111,124
Blasingame, Don: 130,131
Bohne, Sammy: 58,59
Bottomley, Jim: 78
Bowman, Joe: 76
Brainard, Asa: 23
Brennaman, Marty: 13
Bresnahan, Roger: 42,96
Bressler, Rube: 46,62,64,65
Bristol, Dave: 132,136
Brittain, Gus: 80,81
Brosnan, Jim: 128,129
Brown, Joe: 130
Burgess, Smoky: 6,66,116,117
Burkhardt, Ken: 136
Burton, Jim: 146
Bush, Archie: 24
Bush, Owen "Donie": 72
Byron, Bill: 58

C

Camilli, Dolf: 88
Campanella, Roy: 112
Campbell, Bruce: 102
Carbo, Bernie: 146
Carroll, Clay: 9
Caveney, Jimmy: 58
Champion, Aaron: 21
Chandler, A. B. "Happy": 82
Chesbro, Jack: 34
Christensen, Walter "Cookoo": 64
Clemente, Roberto: 144
Cobb, Ty: 40,42,60
Cochrane, Mickey: 72,96
Collins, Dave: 9,43
Comiskey, Charles: 28
Comorosky, Adam: 67

Concepcion, Dave: 9,138,139
Corcoran, Tommy: 138
Corrales, Pat: 136
Cox, George B.: 44
Craft, Harry: 88
Crawford, Sam: 40,41
Critz, Hughie: 26
Crosetti, Frank: 97
Crosley Field: 9,12,14,15,16,33,54,59,
  63,75,87,88,95,102,108,114,122,131
Crosley, Powel: 68,74,75,76,81,82,84,115
Cuccinello, Tom: 96
Cummings, Arthur "Candy": 24,25
Cunningham, Bill: 54
Cuyler, Hazen "Ki-Ki": 84

D

Danning, Harry: 98
Darcy, Pat: 146
Dark, Alvin: 138
Daubert, Jake: 64
Dean, Dizzy: 34
Derrick, Claud: 70
Derringer, Paul: 8,9,16,76,80,81,91,92,93,102
DeWitt, Bill: 120,124,130
Dickey, Bill: 96
DiMaggio, Joe: 24,97
Doby, Larry: 112
Dressen, Charles: 70,80,81,84,136
Driessen, Dan: 132
Durocher, Leo: 88,92,114,134,138

E

Eastwick, Rawly: 142
Eisenhart, Harry: 108
Eller, Horace "Hod": 56,57
Escalera, Nino: 113
Ewing, Buck: 30,31

F

Feller, Bob: 100,110
Ferguson, Jim: 7
Fisk, Carlton: 146
Fleischmann family: 44,70
Fonseca, Lew: 58,72
Ford, Hod: 138
Ford, Whitey: 134
Fosse, Ray: 134,135
Foster, George: 9,138,144
Freese, Gene: 124
Fregosi, Jim: 134
Frey, Lonnie: 142
Frick, Ford: 33,82,83
Fulmer, Charles "Chick": 86

G

Galbreath, John: 82,83
Garagiola, Joe: 136
Gehrig, Lou: 24,106
Gehringer, Charlie: 102

Gelbert, Charley: 92
Gelbert, Wally: 96
Geronimo, Cesar: 144,146
Giles, Warren: 82,83,84,90,94
Giusti, Dave: 144
Goltz, Larry: 114
Goodman, Ival: 97
Gould, Charles H.: 23
Gowdy, Hank: 88
Griffey, Ken: 8,9
Griffith, Clark: 8,76
Grissom, Lee: 14,84,104
Groat, Dick: 130,138
Gross, Don: 126
Grove, Hiney: 9
Grove, Lefty: 88
Gullett, Don: 146
Gumbert, Addison: 28

H

Hahn, Frank "Noodles": 34,35
Hargrave, Eugene "Bubbles": 62,63,64,96
Harmon, Chuck: 112,113
Harrelson, Bud: 134
Harris, Bucky: 72
Hartnett, Gabby: 96
Hassett, Buddy: 88
Hatton, Grady: 6
Helms, Paul Hoy: 32
Helms, Tommy: 26
Hemus, Solly: 128
Henriquez, Dr. Hernandez: 54
Henry, Bill: 128
Herman, Babe: 96
Hernandez, Keith: 148
Herrmann, August "Garry": 38,44,45,46,48,66,72
Hershberger, Willard: 98,99,100
Herzog, Buck: 38,72
Hickman, Jim: 134
Hodges, Gil: 114
Hornsby, Rogers: 62,118
Howsom, Bob: 9,136
Hoy, Carson: 32
Hoy, William E. "Dummy": 32,33
Hoyt, Waite: 106,107,110
Hubbell, Carl: 110
Hurley, Richard: 23
Hutchinson, Fred: 9,122,123,124

I

Irvin, Monte: 112

J

Jay, Joey: 124,125,126
Johnson, Daron: 6
Johnson, Walter: 38
Jones, Bumpus: 28,29
Joost, Eddie: 102

K

Kampouris, Alex: 26,142,143

150

Keller, Charlie: 97
King, Hal: 140,141
Kling, John: 30
Klippenstein, Johnny: 126
Kluszewski, Ted: 6,16,114,115,116
Kopf, Larry: 138
Koosman, Jerry: 148
Koufax, Sandy: 34,126
Koy, Ernie: 88

L

Landis, Judge Kennesaw Mountain: 44
Larsen, Don: 58,59
Lavagetto, Cookie: 88
Lee, Bill: 132,146
LeMaster, Johnnie: 148
Leonard, Andrew: 23
Lockard, Charles: 66
Lombardi, Ernie: 9,62,88,90,96,97,98,100,102
Lucas, Charles Fred "Red": 66,67
Luque, Dolf: 54,55,59

M

Mack, Connie: 94
MacPhail, Larry: 68,69,70,74,76,78,80,81,82
Magee, Lee: 46,50
Maloney, Jim: 34
Mancuso, Gus: 118
Mantle, Mickey: 118
Marquard, Rube: 110
Martin, Billy: 130
Mata, Virgilio: 138
Mathewson, Christy: 34,38,39,40,46,56,86,87
Mattick, Bobby: 112,120,130
Mauch, Gene: 120
May, Milt: 148
Mays, Willie: 112,118
McCarthy, William: 58
McCormick, Frank: 9,78,102
McCosky, Barney: 102
McEnaney, Will: 146
McGraw, John: 36,38,42,48,50,60,66,106,136
McKechnie, Bill: 38,72,82,84,85,86,87,88,89
 90,94,98,100,101,104,108,109,110
McLish, Cal: 124
McMillan, Roy: 124,138
McNamara, John: 9,148
McPhee, Bid: 26,27,28
McQuinn, George: 78
McRae, Hal: 136,144
McVey, Calvin: 23
Menke, Denis: 144
Merriwell, Frank: 67
Meyers, Billy: 102,138
Miller, Eddie: 138
Mitchell, Dale: 58
Mize, Johnny: 78,79
Mollwitz, Fred: 70
Moose, Bob: 144
Moran, Pat: 38,44,46,47,48,62,64
Morgan, Joe: 9,26,132,142,143,146
Morganer, Fred: 7

Mota, Manny: 116
Mullane, Tony: 28
Musial, Stan: 114,135

N

Neale, Greasy: 50
Newcombe, Don: 112
Newsom, Bobo: 92,102
Nuxhall, Joe: 6,9,108,109

O

O'Farrell, Bob: 72,80
O'Toole, Jim: 126

P

Palace of the Fans: 13,14
Patten, Dorcas: 7
Paul, Gabe: 75,98,104,120
Perez, Tony: 9,132,133,144,146,147
Phelps, Babe: 88
Phelps, Blimp: 66
Pinelli, Babe: 56,58,59
Pinson, Vada: 112
Pizarro, Juan: 124
Post, Wally: 116
Purkey, Bob: 126,127

R

Rath, Maury: 46
Redland Field: 14,35,39,43,47,50,51,54,55,76
Reese, Pee Wee: 138
Rickey, Branch: 112
Riggs, Lew: 88,94
Rigler, Cy: 52
Ring, Jimmy: 46
Ripple, Jimmy: 102
Riverfront Stadium: 9,12,16,134,135,137,143,144,146
Rixey, Eppa: 42,53,63
Robinson, Frank: 9,16,112,116,120,121
Robinson, Jackie: 110,112
Rockne, Knute: 42
Rogers, Bill: 58
Rolfe, Red: 61
Rose, Pete: 8,9,16,26,27,36,132,134,135,142,146
Roush, Edd: 8,9,16,38,42,43,46,48,49,50,51,100,118
Ruhl, Roger: 7
Ruppert, Jake: 72
Rusie, Amos: 38
Ruth, Babe: 24,70,71,72,73,106,107,115

S

Sallee, Slim: 46,47
Sanguillen, Manny: 144
Scarsella, Lew: 78
Schalk, Ray: 96
Scheffing, Bob: 124
Schott, Gene: 14
Seaver, Tom: 9,148,149
Sewell, Luke: 83

Sewell, Rip: 146
Seymour, James Bentley "Cy": 36,37
Shore, Ernie: 70
Sisler, Dick: 122,130
Smith, Mayo: 122
Snider, Duke: 118
Spahn, Warren: 52,148
Speaker, Tris: 60
Stallings, George: 54
Stanky, Eddie: 110
Stengel, Casey: 54
Stevens, Harry: 70
Stripp, Joe: 96
Sukeforth, Clyde: 96
Sullivan, Billy: 102
Sutton, Don: 140
Sweasy, Charles: 23

T

Tebbetts, Birdie: 75,115,116,118,121
Temple, Johnny: 26,142
Terry, Bill: 88
Terry, Joe: 66
Thompson, Hank: 112
Thomson, Bobby: 81
Tinker, Joe: 37,70
Tolan, Bobby: 112
Topping, Dan: 68
Twombly, George: 70

V

Valentine, Corky: 112
Vander Meer, Johnny: 9,88,89,90,110
Vargo, Ed: 137
Vergez, Johnny: 90
Virdon, Bill: 138

W

Waddell, Rube: 34
Wagner, Dick: 7,9
Wagner, Hans: 30
Walters, Bucky: 9,16,54,90,91,92,98,100,102
Waterman, Frederick: 23
Weaver, Earl: 120
Webb, Del: 68,82,83
Werber, Bill: 94,95,102
West, Dick: 100
Wilie, Denny: 58
Williams, Ted: 24,114
Wills, Maury: 42
Wilson, Jimmie: 90,91,100,101,102
Woodward, Woody: 138
Wright, Clyde: 134
Wright, George: 9,20,22,23,138
Wright, Harry: 9,20,21,22,23

Y

Yastrzemski, Carl: 146
Young, Cy: 34,148
Young, Ross: 54

151